My Hope
For
The
Church

My Hope
For
The
Church

Critical Encouragement
FOR THE
Twenty-First Century

TRANSLATED BY PETER HEINEGG

LIGUORI/TRIUMPH
LIGUORI, MISSOURI

Published by Liguori/Triumph
An Imprint of Liguori Publications
Liguori, Missouri
http://www.liguori.org

This book is a translation of *Meine Hoffnung für die Kirche: Kritische Ermutigungen*, published by Verlag Herder Freiburg im Breisgau, copyright 1997.

Library of Congress Cataloging-in-Publication Data

Häring, Bernard, 1912–1998.
  [Meine Hoffnung für die Kirche, English]
  My hope for the church : critical encouragement for the 21st century / Bernard Häring ; translated by Peter Heinegg.
      p.   cm.
  Includes index.
  ISBN 0-7648-0379-4
  1. Christian ethics—Catholic authors. 2. Catholic Church—Doctrines. I. Title
BJ1249.H36313   1999
282'.09'049—dc21   98–40685

Scriptural citations are taken from the *New Revised Standard Version of the Bible*, copyright © 1989 by the Division of Christian Education of the National Council of the Churches of Christ in the USA. All rights reserved. Used with permission.

English translation copyright 1999 by Liguori Publications
Printed in the United States of America

03 02 01 00 99   5 4 3 2 1
First Edition in English

Contents

Part II: The Turnaround Looms on the Horizon   89

Foreword

F ather Bernard Häring was the foremost Catholic moral theologian in the twentieth century and a leading advocate for Church reform before, during, and after the Second Vatican Council. He died July 3, 1998, in Gars am Inn, Germany. This volume, the last of over ninety books, can truly be called his last will and testament for the Church he loved and served so wholeheartedly.

The book is vintage Häring. Those who are familiar with his writings will see how he has continued to develop his moral theology and, above all, will appreciate his concrete proposals to overcome the present authoritarian centralization in the Catholic Church. He proposes significant changes in the role of all the people of God, the selection of bishops, and the function of the papacy in the Church. He strongly opposes a controlling centralization in the Church by insisting on the need for inculturation and the diffusion of leadership throughout the people of God by invoking the principle of subsidiarity. This book calls for change in the role of women in the Church, priestly celibacy, and the pastoral care for divorced and remarried Catholics among other issues. Those who have never read Häring will find here an excellent presentation of his approach to moral theology and convincing proposals of the reforms necessary for our Church in the next century.

Who was Bernard Häring? A brief overview of the his life will help the reader appreciate even more what is written in this book.

Häring was born November 10, 1912, the eleventh of twelve children in a pious farm family in southern Germany. He entered the novitiate of the Redemptorist Fathers in 1933 and was ordained a priest in 1939. He had hoped to be a missionary in Brazil, but his superiors wanted him to study moral theology. Häring was very reluctant to study moral theology because he strongly disagreed with the way in which the subject was taught at that time. Thus began the career of the person who became the most significant Catholic moral theologian in the twentieth century!

However, World War II intervened. Häring, who had opposed Hitler, was drafted into the German army as a medic. He regularly disobeyed orders and ministered as a priest to the spiritual needs of soldiers on both sides of the battlefront and to civilians in France, Russia, and Poland. In the process, he faced death many times.

After the war, he finished his doctoral studies in moral theology and taught at the Redemptorist Theologate in Gars am Inn. In 1954, he published his groundbreaking *Law of Christ* calling for a new approach to moral theology. He was appointed to the faculty of the newly established Accademia Alfonsiana in Rome staffed by Redemptorists to teach future professors of moral theology. From 1954 to his retirement in 1986, he was the most influential member of that faculty. Häring was a prodigious author publishing over ninety volumes, including an entirely new three-volume synthesis of moral theology *Free and Faithful in Christ* first written in English in 1979 to 1981.

Häring was also a clear and inspiring lecturer and teacher. He lectured frequently in all parts of the world especially Africa, Asia, Europe, and America, aided by his fluency in German, French, Italian, English, Spanish, Portuguese, and Polish. It is safe to say that no one has spoken personally to more people on this globe about moral theology than Bernard Häring.

From his teaching position in Rome, he influenced the worldwide Church and also played a very significant role in Church reform. Pope John XXIII personally thanked him for his books on moral theology and on the Second Vatican Council. Pope Paul VI in his very first year as pope invited Häring to be his retreat director.

Father Häring made a great contribution to the work of the Second Vatican Council with his work on both preconciliar and conciliar commissions. Cardinal Fernando Cento, the copresident of the mixed commission in charge of the Pastoral Constitution on the Church in the Modern World publicly referred to him as "the quasi-Father" of that document. Häring, as a member of the so-called papal birth control commission, strongly advocated a change in the teaching of the Church. He publicly disagreed with Pope Paul VI's encyclical *Humanae Vitae* which reaffirmed the condemnation of artificial contraception in 1968. The German Redemptorist strongly spoke out against legalism, authoritarianism, overcentralization, the desire to control others, and the lack of trust often found in Church structures and institutions.

In 1980 Häring lost his vocal cords to cancer. He learned to speak from the esophagus, but it was not always easy for him to speak or for others to understand, especially in large numbers. What a cross for one who had truly been a missionary to the whole world through his extraordinarily heavy schedule of lectures and conferences on every continent. In 1986 Häring retired to the Redemptorist Monastery in Gars am Inn, but he continued to write and lecture on occasion. At the end of his autobiography published in English in 1988, Häring wrote: "I contemplate and long for my death as the last, irrevocable, and unsurpassable yes and *amen* to God's salvific will." This statement in German is inscribed on the memorial card commemorating his death.

Häring dramatically changed moral theology by insisting on both a different audience and a different method. The older manuals of moral theology aimed at training priests to become judges in the sacrament of penance with special emphasis on determining what constitutes a sin and the degree of sinfulness. Such an approach was very minimalistic and legalistic.

The Law of Christ in 1954 was written for priests and laity. (Häring later regretted the use of the word "laity" and instead used the phrase "the people of God.") The purpose of his moral theology was to explain all the dimensions of the Christian life and not just the minimum necessary to avoid sin.

Our author insisted on the primary importance of conversion or change of heart as most significant. As the biblical metaphor reminds us, the good tree brings forth good fruit. Good actions come from a good person. He developed a responsibility model of morality based on the Christian's response to God's gracious gift. Häring's understanding of morality was biblically based, rooted in the gracious gift of the Triune God, nourished in the liturgy, and lived out in the world. All his books from the early *Law of Christ* in 1954 to this present volume all illustrate how Häring employed a truly catholic method which recognizes that God is in all things and above all things. He was constantly in ecumenical dialogue with other Christians and also open to the insights of the sociological and psychological sciences.

Häring was not primarily a university scholar writing for a very limited number of academic professionals but a very committed Catholic Christian writing for the people of God. After the Second Vatican Council his many involvements for spiritual renewal and Church reform meant that he could no longer do moral theology with the same depth and creativity, but he continued to develop his basic vision and approach.

This present volume develops his understanding of a holistic moral theology by insisting on the connection between our understanding of God, Church, and the moral life. The morality of the manuals of moral theology saw God as a controller and the Church as a constricting legal institution. Häring's responsibility model (aptly described by the title of his systematic work—*Free and Faithful in Christ*) understands God as the gracious parent and the Church as a community of those who have been saved by God's gracious love through Jesus and the Spirit and are now challenged to live in accord with their new life. This last volume discusses the most vexing questions facing society today—peace, worldwide justice, and responsibility for our endangered planet.

In this volume Häring well illustrates the two characteristics that stand out in his writing and speaking—his frankness and his optimism. This book forcefully criticizes the restorationist mentality at the Vatican at the present time, the claim to have absolute certitude on disputed issues, and the attempt to legalistically enforce conformity. Häring negatively criticizes both the *Catechism of the Catholic Church* and the papal encyclical *Veritatis Splendor*.

Despite his frank opposition to many current structures and approaches, Häring remains optimistic about the future. In the last years of the Wojtyla papacy, the older model has largely run itself into the ground paving the way for a turnaround which is even now in the offing. The second part of this book spells out Häring's realistic dream for a Church which is truly free and faithful. This book clearly provides hope and critical encouragement for the reform of the Church in the twenty-first century.

No one can read the following pages without recognizing Häring's great love for the Church, even when he criticizes it. His own spirituality and commitment also come through in these pages. But to those who had the pleasure of listening to, studying under, or attending spiritual conferences given by Häring, his own spirituality and witness provide the best illustration of a Christian morality that is truly free and faithful.

In conclusion, I must tell the reader that I do not pretend to be a value-free, neutral observer in discussing the work of Bernard Häring. Häring was my teacher, mentor, defender, friend, and director. I will never cease being appreciative of all he has meant to me. For this reason I am all the more grateful for the opportunity to introduce the reader to this last book of Bernard Häring which offers wisdom, hope, and encouragement for all who strive to make ourselves and our Church more faithful to what we are called to be.

CHARLES E. CURRAN
ELIZABETH SCURLOCK UNIVERSITY PROFESSOR OF HUMAN VALUES
SOUTHERN METHODIST UNIVERSITY

Introduction

The first part of this book continues reflections that I presented some time ago in a little volume called *Other Ways of Getting There: Arguments for New Manners in the Church*.[1] Working within a similar framework of discussions on moral theology and the concrete realities of the Church that I began in that book, in this book, I would like to point out the obstacles that are threatening our existence in the Church. Moral theology underwent a unique transformation in the turnaround that was Vatican II, but, more than any other branch of theology, it is also uniquely the target of current conservative efforts to bring about a "restoration." Still, I think I have solid reasons for expressing hope: a powerful turnaround *is* taking place. Old models of the Church are on the decline; new ones are coming into view.

My readers will sense that I don't like it when people put their heads in the sand to avoid seeing the truth. We have to confront the serious problems of this historical moment; but we should not let ourselves be overwhelmed by these problems. We can escape the dangers of pessimism only if we concentrate all our attention on the positive forces that are at work, and thus try to read the signs of the times.

In the second part of the book, I develop the lines of thought sketched out in the first part, and turn to the events and situations that lie beyond discussions of moral theology and that point to new horizons of historical development.

The tremendous new beginning made by the Church in the Second Vatican Council lives on, and not just in our grateful memory. The energies that awakened then are still at work. I see the forces struggling against them as a challenge. Whether or not the current serious crises ultimately prove to be crises of growth depends upon all of us. New things are coming along. There are great opportunities that must not be missed.

Part I

What's at Stake?
New Directions in
Moral Theology and
Restoration of
the Old Order

T he turnaround and new directions in moral theology, as I have experienced them in my life and as I helped to shape them, are accessible to anyone who wants them. At the same time, the new *Catechism of the Catholic Church* and the encyclical *Veritatis Splendor* point toward a restoration of the old order, and they represent a fresh challenge to all of us. They make us ask: What is the issue here? What was at stake and will continue to be at stake for the foreseeable future? Both documents deal not just with a few concrete questions of moral theology, but with the total picture, an overall direction. What is at stake here is the perspective of tomorrow—and the overall context of the future.

At issue, on the one hand, is the interrelation between the self-concept (ecclesiology) and structures of the Church and, on the other hand, the type of moral theology and preaching of morality. What are the connections between ethics and dogma, exegesis, and canon law?

Above and beyond these issues, one vital criterion for the authenticity of the new directions in moral theology was and remains *ecumenism*. We are concerned with reconciling the Christian world, but just as much with reconciling the whole inhabited earth (ecumene). We must aim for the sort of inculturation by which Christian dogma and morality can send down roots everywhere and be the leaven of life. So we must have a concrete realization of catholicity, a unity in fruitful multiplicity.

My particular concern is the relationship of grace and law, as

3

opposed to a kind of moral theology in which grace was only an appendage of the law. Our concern is for the "law of the Spirit of life in Christ Jesus," with radical conversion to the Good News, to life in Christ. We need to have "constant conversion" to a life in keeping with the primitive kerygma: "The time is fulfilled, and the kingdom of God has come near; repent, and believe in the good news" (Mk 1:15).

These questions cannot be dealt with abstractly, in some airless "clean room." They are questions that penetrate deeply into the life of every individual and, needless to say, with particular existential emotion, into the life of moral theology.

1

My Calling As a Moral Theologian

At the beginning of my experiences stands the suffering caused by a certain kind of morality in the Church. I know it was widespread: in preparing for our first confession, we children were given not just precise directions on how to confess absolutely everything, but some violent motivation as well. The parish priest told us about a monk who had died in the odor of sanctity. The abbot had just begun his eulogy after the requiem Mass when a voice boomed from the coffin: "I am damned!" The abbot ordered the dead man under holy obedience to confess the reason for his damnation. Again a hollow voice reverberated from the kingdom of the dead: "Out of shame I concealed a sin at my first confession and never confessed it later." So I worked long and hard to draw up a list of all my sins, certain and supposed, lest the same fate befall me.

Many Catholics from all social classes and conditions have been plagued all their lives by a certain type of moral theology which inspired in them the dread that perhaps they hadn't really confessed all their serious sins. And at that time a person confessing also had to supply exact information about the nature and kind of those sins. Woe to the anxious persons who fell into the hands of a typical "judgmental" confessor. Fortunately, while still a boy I found a confessor who knew how to heal me. Through his whole way of being, he passed on to me a completely different image of

God from that of the clumsy pastor who had borrowed his foolish story, as I later discovered, from a catechetical magazine.

In this context, I had yet another frightening experience. When I was about fifteen years old, my eldest sister delivered twins prematurely. The first twin survived the birth and was given an emergency baptism by the midwife; the second was born dead. The same parish priest who had infected us with such anxiety about an incomplete confession explained to my sister and her husband that only the body of the baptized twin could be buried in consecrated ground. The other baby could not, since he was forever barred from eternal happiness. This decision plunged my sister into deep depression. The whole thing gave me a very sinister feeling, and I wondered—as I told my sister—what sort of image of God was lurking behind our pastor's attitude. Even back then, I was planning on becoming a priest, so I promised myself that one day I would study the whole issue thoroughly. And I did.

The question of a humane image of God tortured me unceasingly later on, when I was studying ethics under a man with a doctorate in both civil and canon law. We had to memorize countless lists of mortal sins incurred by mistakes in performing inconsequential rites. I had an eerie feeling when I heard that a priest who carelessly consecrated hosts in a ciborium not placed on a corporal was committing a serious, that is, a mortal, sin.

Fortunately, around this time I came across the handbook of moral theology by Fritz Tillmann, Theodore Steinbüchel, and Theodore Müncker. It became clear to me that there was a gaping abyss between (among other things) the moral theology they taught and the sort that I known up until then. In conversation with some of my outstanding professors, in particular Father Viktor Schurr, my worries were alleviated, so that I didn't founder in my profession.

Still more: shortly after my ordination the provincial superior came to my room. I was supposed to be getting a ship's passage for Brazil, because the order had long promised that I could work there as a missionary (I had been preparing myself by studying Portuguese). But now the provincial informed me that the faculty—though *not* the moralist just mentioned—had sharply criticized him for wanting to send me to Brazil. Instead, they thought I would do better to specialize in moral theology.

I immediately objected that moral theology, as it had been previously taught, would be my very last choice. But out of obedience I agreed to try it. The superior replied: "That's just the point: they want things to change—radically." And they were confident that I could make a contribution to this change. Given this enormous advance of trust, I said *Yes*. The idea of an "advance of trust" was destined to play a large role in my theology, as it would in my life. I thought of it especially with regard to the salvific action of God: anticipatory grace, the divine advance of trust, became part of the core of my theology and view of the world.

This assignment to study moral theology occurred in the spring of 1939. By the fall, I had been drafted into the medical corps of the Wehrmacht, to serve as a healer in a time of disaster. Shortly before Christmas 1940, thanks to personal connections with a surgeon general, my professors managed to get me a deferment. So, from January to July 1940, I taught moral theology to fellow Redemptorists who were almost as old as I was. Apart from everything else, in view of the dreadful problems of the war and the godless Nazi system, I could never have brought myself to teach along the lines of the Aertnys-Damen manual of moral theology, hitherto the standard text. So, with a pounding heart, I risked taking a whole new approach. Its goal became clear in the final lecture of my course which was given on the subject of "Truth in the Radiance of Love."

Professor Theodore Steinbüchel, a very perceptive man, happened to have taken temporary refuge in Gars (the site of the seminary) from Nazi persecution. He gave me a dissertation topic that, as he said, could serve as a theme for twentieth-century moral theology: "The Holy and the Good" (in other words, the reciprocal relations of faith and morality).

Professor Steinbüchel wanted me to approach this topic from an ecumenical point of view. I tried to do just that, and I learned a great deal in the preparation of that dissertation. I chose Max Scheler to represent the Catholic position, with Friedrich Schleiermacher, Rudolf Otto, and Emil Brunner representing the Protestants. I also studied the Protestant philosopher Immanuel Kant and atheistic phenomenologists, such as Nikolai Hartmann, from Edmund Husserl's school. It was a fascinating task.

But in the fall of 1940, I was called up by the army medical corps again. After a stay in France, I spent the summer of 1941 until the end of the war on the Russian front. I lived in a constant state of tension: summoning up the courage to disobey orders while trying to carry on integral religious work on all levels. As a medic and a chaplain, I was there for both my own comrades and for Russian soldiers and civilians. I led Bible-study evenings with Protestant friends, held ecumenical worship services for various army units—though this was strictly forbidden—and gave pastoral care, as best I could, to Orthodox communities left without a priest. These activities left a permanent mark on me. Thanks to them, there was no way I could ever conceive of a profound renewal of moral theology except ecumenically.

When I unexpectedly returned from Poland (where I had looked after a parish for several months), my superiors insisted I immediately take up my studies again in Tübingen—where in the meantime Theodore Steinbüchel had become a professor of moral theology. When Karl Adam saw me attending one of his courses, he waited for me to come out and warned me not to "waste my precious time" in his class. I was fortunate to be his guest on several occasions, and, earlier, he had sought to convince me to switch over to dogmatic theology, since "there was nothing more to be done" with moral theology. Now he encouraged me to do ecumenical moral theology. I took courses with the most respected Protestant professors: Adolph Köberle, Heinrich Rickert, and Helmut Thielicke. And Professor Steinbüchel, who was my dissertation director, bolstered my ecumenical vocation.

In 1947, I took my Ph.D. with a thesis on "The Holy and the Good." It was published unchanged and found a wide echo in ecumenical circles. This positive response also was an encouragement to me.

It was surely providential that my first students were young men who had been soldiers and, in many cases, prisoners of war in Russia. They were an existential challenge for me to teach a kind of morality that would try to respond to the burning experiences, hopes, and fears of our time.

I got a similar kind of stimulus from my work in the missions for German Catholic refugees. In the early part of my teaching career, during which I wrote *The Law of Christ*, I spent about ten weeks every year in the Catholic diaspora around Coburg and Ansbach. In these regions, which once had been totally Protestant, I went from place to place, preaching to the Catholic wartime and postwar refugees. Sometimes we were the guests in Protestant churches, at other times we rented dance halls.

Before beginning my mission I had sketched out sixteen sermons, but not one of them made it to the pulpit. At each stop along our route, we first visited all the Catholic families so we could hear them out and understand their story. Thus the sermons had to try to match their questions, cares, and expectations. This listening to the people helped me to get some distance from the abstract scholastic language I had learned as a theologian. But it also gradually became clear to me that our moral theology and moral preaching had to reach precisely this sort of person who had been sorely tried by life. And the diaspora situation kept my ecumenical concerns alive.

Meanwhile, I also had a crucial experience in Rome with the founding of the Accademia Alfonsiana. Back in 1948, during his visit to Germany the superior general, Leonardus Buys, a Dutchman, called me in for a long discussion. He invited me to spend a semester in Rome as part of his plan to found an institute for the training of future professors of moral theology. His thinking was based on an experience that both of us found distressing: up until then, it was common practice for superiors and bishops all over the world to send young priests to Rome to study canon law. When they had completed their studies, these newly formed canon lawyers were often appointed as professors of moral theology. It was clear to us that canon law, even in conjunction with civil law, could not be an appropriate background for the teaching of Christian ethics, of truly Catholic moral theology.

After long conversations, the superior general asked me to present my concerns about the training of future moral theologians in a talk before the General Conference and other interested parties. I used drastic language: we had to put a stop to the dangerous concubinage with canon law, where morality was notoriously dominated by law. We had to go back to an integral theology, to a chaste marriage, where the word of God showed the way to a faith that bore fruit in love, justice, and peace. I stressed the importance of the social sciences in the constant effort to achieve a knowledge of human beings that was historically accurate and in line with each particular culture.

At the same time, I used my time in Rome to see how they taught morality in the various Roman colleges. I will never forget a class I visited at the Gregorian University. In a giant hall, Father

F. X. Hürth, one of the chief editors of the encyclical *Casti Connubii,* was lecturing in fluent Latin to a group of attentive and amazed students. The case in point was as follows: a priest comes into an area with no other priests. May he celebrate Mass twice on a workday, if otherwise a whole parish would have to go without Mass for a long time? To this day I can hear Hürth's emphatic answer, which sent a shiver down my spine: "Absolutely not! There is not now and never has been a law requiring the celebration of Mass on a workday!"

I looked around, expecting an uproar, but there was nothing of the sort. As a farm boy, I had learned from my father not to harness a horse by starting with the tail. So was it the law and nothing but the law when it came to the Eucharist? In this light, I now read the handbooks of moral theology that dealt with the sacraments according to the countless commandments and laws. These manuals asked: what help were the sacraments in fulfilling the laws?

In 1950, the first courses began at the Accademia Alfonsiana, at first just for Redemptorists and a few Dutch secular priests. By arrangement with the superior general of the Redemptorists, my first offerings were (1) "Continuous Conversion As a Core Dynamic of Christian Morality" and (2) "What Can Catholic Moral Theology Learn From Orthodox and Lutheran Theologians?"

The course on conversion as a key to moral theology was well received. The other course stirred up a lot of interest, but some people were shocked that I said nothing polemical whatsoever about theologians from other faiths. For them, the transition from the theology of controversy to a theology of ecumenical dialogue was too abrupt. I asked my listeners to attend a few lectures at the Biblicum by Professor Stanislas Lyonnet, who just then was teaching a course on grace and law in Paul, a topic in which I was deeply interested. My students noted that Lyonnet and I had the same intonation, the same concern, and the same accent.

It proved to be very much an advantage in the following years that, as my work on *The Law of Christ* progressed, I had to teach both the "old warriors" in Gars and the future professors in Rome. I got a great deal of encouragement from both groups.

Over the course of the years, I saw with increasing clarity the link between the predominant image of the Church on the one hand and the Church's morality on the other. My experience of the Second Vatican Council deepened and enlivened this reciprocity. Very early on, it was plain to me that the hopeful attempts at renewal of moral theology by Johann Michael Sailer, Johann Baptist Hirscher, and Franz Xavier Linsenmann in Germany had been doomed to failure. This was because, first, they moved exclusively in a German milieu, but still more because the harsh winds of the Church's shift toward restoration were blowing in their faces. If one wished to work for the renewal of moral theology, it wasn't enough to make sure that it was nurtured by the Word of God, important as that is. Nor was it enough to do everything possible to get to know humans better in their historical, cultural, and psychic makeup. One also had to be fully aware that the moral theology taught by the Roman school in the legalistic manuals was a mirror image of the post-Tridentine centralized Church. That was where the great nineteenth-century German reformers of moral theology had come a cropper.

For my work, *The Law of Christ*, which even before the Council had been translated into ten languages, an ecumenical concept of the Church, stood sponsor, at least in part. But this thinking still largely mirrored the Roman Catholic Church of the time—as shaped in Rome and by Rome.

I wrote nothing in *The Law of Christ* that I believed to be false. But, on the other hand, I passed over in silence many points I thought were true, because they would have been just too much to ask of influential church leaders. And unconscious self-censorship also played a role here. I did not yet have the courage to look all these questions in the eye and give them an unflinching answer.

For myself, as for many theologians and bishops, the Council was an eyeopener, particularly in regard to the connection between the image of the Church (including church structures) and moral theology. The most influential men in and around the Holy Office spontaneously sensed that *The Law of Christ* did not fit their notion of the Church. They could see that this sort of morality called for a thorough scrutiny of ecclesiology and the structures of the Church. When these men failed to exclude me from the preparatory commission, they were implacably determined to keep me off the subcommission on morality—until Pope John XXIII personally intervened.

Two draft statements, one on the moral order and one on chastity, marriage, and virginity had already been worked out. When the commission had to call me in, it was quite clear what sort of notions about the Church lay behind these draft statements. They corresponded exactly to the drafts proposed by the preparatory commission on the Church. One of the first jobs of the conciliar commission on faith and morals was to produce a new draft on the doctrine of the Church. This draft began—as in the definitive text of *Lumen Gentium*—with a discussion of the Church as the people of God on pilgrimage, as a fellowship of salvation, and so on. Only afterward does the text speak of the offices and services in the Church.

On this commission, Cardinal Alfredo Ottaviani embodied Rome's traditional notion of itself. As he admonished me on at least three occasions: "You've got to speak first about the Church and only then about the Church's subordinates." The future Cardinal Joseph Schröffer kept trying to explain to Ottaviani that the pope and the Vatican are part of the Church, too. They belong to the people of God; they are not and cannot be "the Church" all by themselves.

2

The Great Turnaround and the Driving Force of the New Directions—A Preeminent Turning to the Word of God

The epoch-making turnaround in Catholic moral theology would have been unthinkable without the renewal of Scripture studies. We have to thank a whole generation of exegetes for this groundbreaking work. Despite all the sanctions placed on them by the Vatican, they showed their absolute loyalty to the Church in the honesty and thoroughness of their work. In that way, they made it possible for biblical scholarship to be confirmed under Pius XII in the encyclical *Divino Afflante Spiritu (Inspired by the Holy Spirit)*.

One man to whom our generation of moral theologians owes a great debt of gratitude was Fritz Tillmann, who had given up exegesis as the result of pressure from the Vatican, but he had made his presence felt in a revitalized kind of moral theology. His *Handbook of Catholic Ethical Teaching*,[2] produced in collaboration with Theodore Steinbüchel and Theodore Müncker, gave us younger theologians the courage to rethink our positions. Tillmann's work took on crucial importance because it did not offer a substitute for traditional confessor's manuals. Instead, it sought to orient

Christian morality on a high level, yet in simple terms. It clearly showed us—and here one could see that *this* was how Tillmann bade farewell to exegesis—how fruitful the moral message of the New Testament could be for our lives. With the tools of scholarly exegesis, he could tie in with the efforts of Johann Michael Sailer and Johann Baptist Hirscher, whose goal had been to present the full ideal of Christian life, a morality based on the Gospel.

I tried to continue building on this foundation and to gain a wider audience for these ideas. I wanted to synthesize the new approach of Tillmann and the basic issues of the moral theology practiced over the last three centuries. But I tried to avoid the impression of a radical break with the past. This was a difficult transition, with all the advantages and disadvantages of any such gradual changeover.

My language in *The Law of Christ* likewise had a somewhat contradictory appearance. On the one hand, I had picked up from Tillmann and other respected exegetes the grand lines of holy Scripture. On the other, when it came to concrete individual issues, I fell back on the old method of using proof texts for statements by the Church, without quite realizing the problems caused by this traditional model. That does not mean that I always felt comfortable with it. So, in the following editions, I tried to investigate more critically whether Holy Scripture really said the things for which I had cited it as proof. I had to work long and hard to rethink and, where necessary, restructure what I had been taught; this task could be discouraging, but it was challenging, too.

From the very beginning, in the Accademia Alfonsiana program, distinctly new directions were explored on the subject of Scripture and its "reception": a chair for New Testament exegesis was made an integral part of its course of studies. Beyond that, I insisted on the founding of a chair for Old Testament and the appointing of a good candidate to it; once again, my goal was to turn moral theology around. We were greatly helped on this score by the friendly ties we had with the Biblical Institute in Rome. Many of our students attended lectures there, too, and in the early years we maintained a steady exchange of ideas with the faculty of the Biblicum.

The Second Vatican Council was supremely important for the turnaround in moral theology. Still, I think that the efforts to create a new moral theology *before* the Council helped to create a breakthrough and achieve a fresh understanding at the Council. Nevertheless, we largely have the Council to thank that this change in morality, which was both broad and deep, managed to prevail and achieve solidification.

Some decisive factors in this turnaround were found carefully articulated in the two constitutions *Lumen Gentium* and *Gaudium et Spes*—the concept of the Church and the impulses to reform churchly structures. All these new approaches, however, did not take place without a few dubious compromises with the old school.

The clearest reflection of the rethinking process, however, may be found in the Decree on Ecumenism. In it, one no longer hears the voice of a Church that feels obliged to take refuge in a sort of stronghold. This is no longer a Church defending its claim to full possession of all the truths of salvation and all moral directives in opposition to the other branches of Christendom. The age of fruitless controversies has now ended. At the center of the Church, as renewed by the Council, we now find the concern of its divine Founder that "All may be one."

The Church once more wished to breathe "with both lungs," as Pope Paul VI states. Once again, the realization dawns that we cannot do without the spirituality of the Eastern Churches. Their synodal structure holds up to us the mirror of an older tradition and constitution, which is common to the entire Church. Like-wise, biblically oriented Christian ethics, with its concern for "free-dom in Christ," which was one of the great goals of the Reformed Churches, is now close to our hearts.

As far as the renewal of moral theology per se was concerned, a sharp confrontation broke out in the preparatory commission for faith and morals between those who supported the legalistic Roman moral theology and those for whom new departures or turnarounds were imperative. This could be seen in two docu-ments "On the Moral Order" and one on chastity, marriage, and the family. When I was brought in as a coworker and read these already finished drafts, I realized what was really at stake in these two documents: the whole issue of a turnaround in moral theol-ogy and, still more, the Church's self-concept.

I took a point-for-point position on the documents and man-aged to introduce a large number of modifications. A typical mo-ment in this situation came when a member of the subcommission who favored church reform gave me an urgent bit of advice: I would do better, he said, to leave the whole thing as it was. Only then could we be confident that the drafts would be rejected by the Council. Whereas if we cleaned up the most offensive pas-sages, many Council Fathers might not immediately see whose side these drafts were on. Nevertheless, they were sent to all Coun-cil participants in a toned-down version.

In the period that followed, I had an opportunity to present my case before a large number of bishops, particularly from Africa. I began with a line from Paul Claudel: "Yes, we love Christ. But nothing in the world could move us to love this kind of morality." And so, in the end, these texts, so typical of the narrow-minded Roman approach to moral theology, were tabled.

When the vote was taken in the plenary session on the draft of the decree *Optatam Totius* (Decree on Training of Priests), there was a storm of petitions demanding a clear statement against legalistic narrowness in moral education. The commission in charge invited me to compose a brief text in response to these petitions. I advised the commission not to issue any condemnations of the traditional morality of the Roman school.

I proposed, instead, a constructive thesis, which was almost unanimously approved in the subsequent plenary vote. It can be found in n. 16 of the decree: "In like manner, the other theological subjects should likewise be revised on the basis of a more vivid contact with the mystery of Christ and the history of salvation. Special care should be given to the perfecting of moral theology. Its scientific presentation should draw more fully on the teaching of holy Scripture and should throw light on the exalted vocation of the faithful in Christ and their obligation to bring forth fruit in charity for the life of the world. In the same way, the teaching of canon law and church history should take into account the mystery of the Church...." In the light of this statement, holy Scripture must not be simply a collection of evidence for ethical and ecclesial norms, but our basic nourishment, with the whole of its expressive power.

The issue in these words is the nobility of our vocation in Christ: hence the clear allusion to the Pauline and Johannine view of "life in Christ." This opened the way for the New Testament view of the "law of the Spirit of life in Christ Jesus" and "bearing fruit in love." Standardization was not the key here, but *paraclesis*, encouragement in the power of the Holy Spirit to bring forth fruits worthy of repentance, of life in Christ.

It's worth noting that in this context the Council also made a statement about the basic orientation of canon law, which is supposed to express the Church's self-concept.

It should also be mentioned that, in its process of renewal, moral theology was helped a great deal by the constitution *Dei Verbum* (Dogmatic Constitution on Divine Revelation), especially the relationship between Scripture and living tradition.

The pastoral constitution *Gaudium et Spes* calls for thinking that is true to life and focused on the history of salvation.[3]

Immediately after the end of the Council, my French publisher printed the eighth edition of *The Law of Christ* unchanged, without informing me beforehand, casually remarking: "Since the Council has admitted that Father Häring is right, we can simply reprint him." This action irritated me because I had never thought that there was nothing or very little to be learned from the Council.

The eighth edition of the German-language *The Law of Christ* was also due to be released. I wished to incorporate the lessons from Vatican II in this edition, so I took great pains to revise the entire text in the light of the Council, above all on the use of Scripture. Many sections were completely rewritten. Still, I have to admit that in a lot of ways this revision left me dissatisfied. The Council had opened new horizons to us and encouraged us to become a learning community in frankness and honesty. However, it wasn't until 1974 that I decided to risk a new synthesis in the light of the Council and postconciliar experience.

3

Turning to a New Audience

The audience for traditional Roman morality was the confessor, generally understood as the judge in the confessional. This morality was clerical. The "lay person" was plainly called "my child"; the penitent got his or her guidelines from the priest in the sacrament of penance and in the life of the Church as a whole.

After the turnaround, moral theology has ceased to be a morality of the confessional. This is *not* to degrade the importance of the sacrament of penance (or rather of reconciliation). But it puts the sacrament into a different context.

In the subtitle of one of his works, J. M. Sailer stresses that he is speaking not just to theologians, but also to educated lay people. Borrowing from Sailer, I gave *The Law of Christ* the subtitle "Moral Theology for Priests and Lay People." Nowadays, I consider the expression "lay people" unfortunate, though at the time it was aimed at the old clericalism. At issue is purely and simply the Christian in the present, the Christian in the world and the Church, the "grown-up Christian."

To Whom Does the Moral Theologian Listen?

This question is an indispensable prelude to the next, namely, who is the audience of moral theology. We need only say that

20

listening to the word of God is the basic presupposition of all theology. But, in heeding the words of Scripture, we will not make much progress unless we are listeners on the horizontal level.

I myself was first a listener in the circle of my family, where I found no gap between word and life, but a vital, mutual listening. My parents took our questions seriously. I can still hear the echo in my ears—or rather, my heart—of something my mother often said. In the time after the First World War, there were many beggars. If one of them came just before dinnertime, my mother would affably tell him: "Today you are our guest." And there was no condescension in those words.

Later, when I was in Russia and trying my best to serve the people, I asked a young woman teacher how they had explained the Jesus-prayer to her. She told me the following story:

> At the beginning of advent, Pyotr said to his children: "On Christmas Eve Jesus will visit us." They asked, "What does he look like?" And the reply came, "I do not know. But you might be blind and not recognize him. So pray without ceasing: Jesus, son of David, Jesus Son of God, have mercy on me. Don't let me be blind." On Christmas Eve, someone knocked at the door. Pyotr ran and opened it. A nasty smell poured into the room. There was a beggar in rags and full of sores. Pyotr welcomed him with reverence, washed him and bound up his wounds and sores, and gave him a new suit of clothes. He set him down at the table and served him supper. Then his children came and asked: "Papa, when is Jesus coming?" Pyotr started crying: "Children, are you still blind? Didn't you pray rightly?"

If we are not prepared to honor Christ in the least of our brothers and sisters, we will never rightly understand his good news for the poor, for us poor. Moral theologians have to pay special attention to those who seem to have no voice before the world. If their heart, their love of Jesus, is with the littlest, the despised, the morality they teach will become a proclamation for the despised, the marginalized, the "unclean" of every sort. If they compose a morality for the educated, it will be Christian only to the extent that they look upon the least of their brethren with the eyes of Jesus, and always have them in mind when they speak.

Needless to say, Catholic moral theologians listen to the pope, but not in the sense of an isolated voice. They will listen to him all the more when the pope is really the voice of the college of bishops, indeed the voice of the whole people of God as well. At the same time, the pope should also set an example in listening to the voice of Jesus by paying special heed to the cry of the "least."

Moral theologians will unerringly find and get through to their audience if they open themselves to the magisterium of the saints, the peacemakers, those who heal through nonviolence, and win a hearing for them with their readers and listeners. All moral theologians must, to be sure, bear their own personal responsibility. They can do this properly only through living dialogue with the community of moral theologians beyond the frontiers of their own country—with all of theology, insofar as they can participate in it.

Who Is the Audience for Moral Theologians?

The immediate audience of moral theological discourse may well be priests and future pastoral caregivers. But no moral theologian should shape morality with an exclusive view to those entrusted with pastoral care or otherwise responsible for others. In the Middle Ages and early modern period, good theologians wrote "Mirrors of Princes" to sharpen the conscience of monarchs. Hence, along with general morality, which aims to say the essential things for everyone, there is a need for professional ethics for doctors, nurses, and medical caregivers, for jurists, and the men and women in the communications industry—without narrowing the horizon in any way. Moral theologians and ethicists must have breadth; they must have many "antennas." For all their specialization, they must see the whole picture.

If moral theologians seriously aim for this breadth and closeness to human beings, they will never turn into mindless "standardizers." As that breadth and closeness grow, they will be more aware of their own limits. They will be less and less inclined to be "absolutists," without, of course, falling into an empty relativism. But as soon as they stop being listeners and learners, they will have lost their vocation. History, real life, will go right over their heads or pass them by. They will miss their audience, unless they constantly strive to be an audience for all men and women.

4

Turning Away From Laws and Commandments to the "Law of the Spirit of Life in Christ Jesus"

T he traditional manuals of Roman moral theology never denied the necessity of grace. But, in their overall structure and focus, they subordinated grace to the law. Grace appeared mainly as a means: it was needed to observe the law.

In a truly Christian morality, by contrast, grace and the gift of freedom, for which Christ has liberated us, are absolutely set over commandment and law. Grace and freedom are the source, the center of meaning, and the goal. That doesn't mean a weakening of law and order. But if one views the law wholly from the perspective of the grace and glory of the *covenant*, then it has another value altogether.

Paul, who struggles so mightily against turning the proclaiming of salvation into legalism, praises the "law of the Spirit of life in Christ Jesus" (Rom 8:2). The power of the grace of the Holy Spirit sets us free, and not just from all servitude to human laws and compulsions. Above all, it shows us the way to follow in the imitation of Jesus, who is the life, truth, path, and goal of our life. One has to see the radical otherness of the concept of law. When

Paul speaks of the "law of Christ" (Gal 6:2), he means above all the power of the Holy Spirit that makes it possible to fulfill the command of Christ to love one another as he has loved us.

Thus the New Testament's concept of law univocally refers to being in Christ, understood as being truly free. Paul speaks to Christians who are aware of being and living in Christ Jesus (Rom 8:1). Dyed-in-the-wool selfishness has no power over them anymore: "For the law of the Spirit of life in Christ Jesus has set you free from the law of sin and death" (Rom 8:2) Free through Christ and with Christ, we have been liberated from the deadly power of solidarity in disaster (*hamartia*).

In this context, there are two basic features of the turnaround in moral theology, with its stress on the Bible and salvation history: first, the unmasking of deadly legalism, which drives us into slavery and fear; second, and still more, the emphasis on the liberating and healing power of the "law of the Spirit in Christ Jesus."

In the section that follows we confront the double question: from what and for what has Christ freed us? I shall try to work out the answer with a view to the New Testament and to the basic experiences of both the turnaround in Catholic moral theology and the especially urgent concerns of today.

Liberated From the Fascination With Imposed Laws

In his encyclical *Veritatis Splendor (Splendor of Truth)*, John Paul II gives a impressive list (though it makes no claim to completeness) of seriously binding prohibitions; every one of them is absolute and without exception. It is true that in the post-Tridentine period by no means all moralists have stressed so unequivocally the absolute rigidity of moral laws. But the number of laws and condemnations binding under serious sin was enormous.

Add to that the massive threat of eternal punishment in hell for every more or less voluntary trespass, and a tremendous, paralyzing potential for anxiety might develop. But, beyond that, all the available attention of Christians was fascinated and monopolized by this multitude of menacing laws and bans. In the end there was scarcely any creative energy left for constructive, liberating, and healing action.

The problem wasn't simply, however, the sheer number of laws, the violation of which supposedly threatened one's salvation. It was still more the obsessively heavy accent on the ritual and sexual sector.

The turnaround of moral theology in the last forty years has a very different set of emphases. The disciples of Christ are to seek happiness and fascination in the beatitudes and the sublime "target commandments." They are to be constantly given fresh encouragement (*paraclesis*) to let themselves be filled with enthusiasm by Christ, the way, the truth, and the life.

They are further asked to realize that no one must cover the whole way at once. We only have to take the steps that are possible and helpful in any given situation. The main thing is to be going more and more clearly in the right direction.

The Crucial Point: Less Avoidance of Sin Than Solidarity in Salvation

The discussions marking the turnaround in moral theology on the basic option (which *Veritatis Splendor* completely misunderstands) are not primarily aimed at judging individual acts. Above all, they focus not on an individualistic notion of freedom, but on the decision for salvific solidarity in Christ and with all people. And this decision is not made once and for all but made over and over.

Part of the liberating basic option is its constantly growing rootedness in the ensemble of key attitudes and values. "For the love of Christ urges us on, because we are convinced that one has died for all; therefore all have died. And he died for all, so that those who might live no longer for themselves, but for him who died and was raised for them" (2 Cor 5:14–15).

What's at Stake? Not Just My Freedom but the Liberation of Everyone

Those who think only of their own freedom are and remain slaves of egoism. They are vulnerable to every form of collective enslavement because they have opted for the slave's individualism. Once we are freed by Christ *from* slavery to sin, we have been set free *for* the kingdom of love and peace. This means, in particular, that we live in imitation of the nonviolent Servant of God, who is accessible to us on all levels, for healing, liberating, and reconciling love.

Anyone who wants to test church documents and publications on moral theology for their fidelity to the new direction, must ask first and foremost how these materials rate healing and liberating nonviolence. I myself have carefully read through the entire new *Catechism of the Catholic Church* to check this point. The result, to my mind at least, was not very satisfying: nonviolence is anything but a persistent motif there.

A Question Always of Both Liberation and Healing

When touched by the Gospel of freedom in Christ, we become increasingly more aware that we are neither quite free nor quite whole. If we make a radical commitment to the liberating and healing message of the Gospel, we vividly realize that we are at best "wounded healers," in need of healing and liberation our-selves. But that *doesn't* mean we should stand aside until we are altogether whole and free. On the contrary: only through our mutual efforts, brave yet humble, will we be on the right path to the freedom and fullness of salvation for which Christ has set us free.

Free From Paralyzing Fear, Free to Trust

Whatever one thinks of the controversial German psycholo-gist-theologian Eugen Drewermann, nobody can simply ignore his warnings about the anxiety created by religion. In almost all religions, including Catholic Christianity, there was and still is a temptation to use the potent motive of fear, forcing people to toe the line in religion and other things. It is a satanic notion to ex-ploit the name of God and Christ to make people submissive through feelings of anxiety, even if this exploitation is for noble causes.

There is, to be sure, a "fear of God" that can be salutary and healing. But it must be, as Augustine says, a "chaste fear." He compares this feeling of chaste fear to a wife who doesn't want to provoke her husband's justified displeasure with the "unchaste fear" of an unfaithful wife who only worries about being unmasked or punished.

The old, narrow-minded confessional morality with its hun-dreds of threats of mortal sin and its booming sermons on hell, has driven many people into neurotic anxiety and paralyzed their attempts to do good. For Christians, the liberation from fearful-ness, anxiety, and tormenting concerns for one's own salvation awakens new dimensions of freedom, liberation, and healing. It gives us a new élan for a grateful and magnanimous love.[4]

Neurotic anxiety, injected through teaching, structures, and behavior, along with associated fearful expectations, all too often block the way to true freedom. In fact, they make it extremely hard to keep the negative commandments. Amazingly enough, some fanatical spokesmen of the old casuistry seem totally unaware of this connection. Don't they know about the progress made by the social sciences? Are they so hopelessly stuck in the old ruts?

Being caught up in fear of a terrifying, menacing God stifles us. In both Church and society, it throttles the healing and liberating energies of openness, of which, for example, the Acts of the Apostles speak with such eloquence and enthusiasm.

Many hostilities and even the cruelest wars have been at least partly caused by sick fear, anxiety and mistrust.

Religion often invests deeply in feelings of anxiety and guilt complexes. In so doing, it robs itself—however many calls for peace it may issue—of the fulfillment of its grand responsibility to work for peace and reconciliation.

Free From Hesitancy, Empowered for Frankness

The primitive Church manifested the freedom of Christ in an astonishing frankness (*parrhesia*) after the model of the Divine Master. Frankness is one of the clearest signs of the Pentecost experience, the outpouring of the Holy Spirit, about which Peter speaks so vividly on the very feast of Pentecost: "Even upon my slaves, both men and women, in those days I will pour out my Spirit" (Acts 2:18).

Without such Pentecostal frankness, we cannot imagine reevangelization—the ongoing proclamation of salvation in a rapidly changing world and in cultures where manipulators have an easy time with overwhelming numbers of fearful, characterless, and intellectually uniformed personalities. Those who are now trying to restore the old moral theology, who are trying to achieve total uniformity, who see divergent thinking and free speech as the great danger, must be holding their breath.

I believe that there are many nervous individuals who for security's sake prefer to stick with the restoration party rather than with other trends such as liberation theology. Such nervousness might be helped if people realized that true liberation always goes hand in hand with healing and with nonviolence, and that liberation is absolutely unthinkable without freedom of speech.

Free From the Addiction to Centralizing Control, Free for Collegiality

The Church of Vatican II sees itself as a sacrament of unity, of peace, and cooperation on the way of salvation. Hence, in its structures and structurally conditioned relations, the Church must be a fountainhead of health. It must be a model of sound and healing relations, an advanced and uniformly comprehensible school of relational therapy.[5]

The Temptation of Centralism

History shows us that centralized forms of domination are highly vulnerable to the uncontrolled exercise of power, which wants to keep everything except itself under control. Absolute rulers and dictators compensate for their inner uncertainty and ever-present fear of losing absolute power by concentrating still more power in their hands. To do so, they need compliant officials, agents with broad authority, and that, in turn, strengthens the anxiety over power and influence among this small inner circle.

Consider the emergence of absolutist empires, for example in Mesopotamia, Egypt under Alexander the Great and the Diadochi, or the Roman Empire: centralism and the tendency to expansion through war are closely linked. The monopoly of power in a single bloc leads to abuse and violence.

With the papacy, too, centralization was often accompanied by involvement in the power struggles of earthly kingdoms. The persecution of witches and the bonfires of the Inquisition were not originally the work of the popes. They were the result of collective neurotic anxieties for which they served as means to secure power.

Unfortunately, when Garibaldi and the Italian state, in its quest for national unity, deprived the popes of their temporal power, the Church's leadership didn't immediately see this as liberation and relief from a burden. Many commentators have suspected that the centralistic view of the Vatican's supreme jurisdiction and of papal infallibility may be at least partly explained by the still recent wound from the loss of secular power.

In any event, by now the firm conviction has prevailed that the Church should not get mixed up in power politics, nor should it be organized in its own religious territory along centralistic, absolutistic lines of domination. History has given us clear insights into the ways absolutistic centralization in the Roman Catholic Church matched the absolutistic government of France during the time of the "Babylonian" exile in Avignon. (And this period has to be seen within the overall context of Constantinian power structures and developments.)

It is obvious that there was an all too worldly kind of assimilation, with many far-reaching consequences. These went far beyond church structures, and some of them stubbornly persist to this day. Clericalism and naive thinking about ideologies of power marched in lockstep. The rise of the mendicant orders led by Saint Francis of Assisi and Saint Dominic was a prophetic, loving, and nonviolent protest. Regrettably not everyone understood and followed it.

A Brotherly and Sisterly Primitive Church As a Model

It goes without saying that a global Church cannot follow the model of the primitive Church down to the slightest details. Nevertheless, the ideal picture of the brotherly and sisterly primitive Church, with its collegial and subsidiary forms, must always be kept in mind. We need it as a corrective to the later historical developments that took a completely opposite tack.

How carefully Peter went to work in choosing Matthias to replace Judas. He did take the initiative; he did see the necessity of doing something. But the names submitted for the position came from the whole community. And finally the decision between the two candidates was made not by Peter's authoritarian *Yes* or *No*, but by lot.

A similarly collegial procedure was followed with the introduction of deacons and the choice of appropriate individuals. And the relations of the primitive Church of Jerusalem with the sister churches founded by Paul and other apostles were distinctly collegial, based on dialogue, brotherly and sisterly, in full reciprocity.

The Appointment of Bishops: A Key Problem

For the first thousand years not one pope—no bishop of Rome—ever thought he had the right to appoint bishops everywhere. These appointments, or rather elections, took place according to the principle of subsidiarity—unless the emperor or other secular rulers interfered. Even in the controversy over investiture under Gregory VII, the point at issue was not the centralism favored by the pope, but the independence of the Church, and especially the bishops, from secular control.

Rome took away from the Catholic emperors and kings the

often highly dangerous habit of interfering with the rights of the Church by proposing or simply appointing bishops dependent upon the throne. The popes basically wanted to protect the autonomy of the Church's domain. But in the final analysis it was this very will that continually cut back on and repressed the autonomy of the eastern Churches.

Nowadays the high number of bishops that have to be chosen or appointed every year should make us realize how crucial it is to return to a open and aboveboard subsidiarity.

The Church's Concentration of Power: A Risk

Let's imagine that there has been an unfortunate papal election—there have been more than a few of those in history—and, furthermore, that this sort of pope has been ruling for twenty-five years as he pleased. In that case, he would have chosen slavishly dependent coworkers, and named bishops, cardinals, and theologians to meet his own criteria. Every misguided appointment of a bishop by Rome reflects badly on the prestige of the papacy and harms the trusting relations between Rome and the local churches. One need only point to the man named to succeed Helder Camara.

Such pronunciamentos are no model for healthy, healing relations and structures. The more intense the centralized decision-making is, the more it promotes mechanisms of control that go hand in hand with fear and mistrust. The firmer the centralization, the more the spirit of responsibility, which should flourish on all levels and favor healthy relations, is stopped dead in its tracks.

Centralistic control over whole sections of the global Church presupposes or promotes an all too vigorous self-confidence on the part of the controllers. There is no avoiding the fact: behind all efforts at centralization lies a lack of trust that the Spirit of God wishes to work in and through everyone.

5

Collegiality and Subsidiarity

Many alert Catholics sat up and were shocked to hear press reports of a synod of bishops at which the *circulus latinus* (the discussion group of curial cardinals and their immediate coworkers) tore into the principle of subsidiarity. While the Church had continuously preached subsidiarity as part of its social doctrine, the *circulus latinus* opposed its use as a fundamental principle of order in the Church.

The synodal documents plainly expressed a wish to study whether the principle of subsidiarity also applied to the constitution of the Church. Well, as long as a problem is only "under study," any application of subsidiarity can be blocked or canceled. But then what happens to the credibility of this sort of Church and, in particular, of its social teaching?

Without respect for the principle of subsidiarity, there is no real collegiality. Speaking of the tendency to twist the Council's statements on collegiality to favor unlimited centralization by a papal "government," Karl Rahner energetically remarked some time ago: "Practically speaking, isn't the authority and initiative of the college of bishops reduced to a merely verbal fiction, if at any time the pope can prevent it from taking effect? It doesn't take a long explanation to see that this second question is no doubt the crucial one in any ecumenical dialogue about the primacy and the synodal structure of the Church."[6]

When it comes to the use of the principle of subsidiarity as a structural maxim of the Church, nothing less than everything is at stake: brotherliness and sisterliness in the highest degree of openness to the Holy Spirit, the indispensable willingness to learn of the entire pilgrim people, maximum readiness to listen and learn on the part of those who bear the greatest responsibility in the Church.

6

From the Ethics of Obedience to the Ethics of Responsibility: A Paradigm Change

T
here has been a clear-cut and consistent paradigm change from a one-sided ethic of obedience for the "subjects" of the Church to a bold ethic of responsibility for grown-up Christians. This is indeed one of the key signs of the turnaround in moral theology over the last four decades.

At the Second Vatican Council, this changeover was enshrined, above all, in the pastoral constitution *Gaudium et Spes*. The ethic of responsibility, practically and theoretically, as compared with the ethic of obedience, is in my eyes the clearest shibboleth. It is the sign acknowledging an authentic changeover in a renewed moral theology; and that applies equally to the supporters of a restoration of old-style moral theology.

A genuine ethic of responsibility embraces, purifies, and ennobles obedience. This applies, above all, to the obedience of faith, that is, the sincere, believing attention to the Word of God, the group effort to listen to and look for the signs of the times. The ethic of responsibility takes shape and proves itself in the mutuality of obedience, of listening to one another.

The people most appropriate for leadership roles in society

and the Church are those who have the keenest ear for listening to and empathizing with others. The Latin phrase *ob-auditus fidei*, the obedience of faith, expresses the role of listening as a basic mode of true obedience.

Such listening is also the source of the capacity for responsibility. How can people answer and show a true-to-life responsibility with their entire existence if they cannot really listen? And people who themselves don't listen are ultimately not listened to. Obedience and responsibility, if they are authentic, are designed for reciprocity.

In setting up and scrutinizing norms, a scholarly ethic of responsibility will inevitably pay a lot of attention to the foreseeable consequences of any given norm. This is called the *teleological* aspect of establishing norms. Traditional teleology has nothing to do with calculating practical usefulness. But it must, keeping in mind both the general norm and the concrete action, consider whether and how such an action "benefits" the overall good of individuals and the community. Does a norm contribute to the flourishing of peace, mutual trust, solidarity in action, maturity of character, and so on?

"Deontological norming" stresses the general principles, for example, of natural law; but even these cannot be fully understood without heeding the "telos," the goal of the norm itself. If one were to lose sight of the goal, deontology could also serve the cause of mechanization and mere slavish obedience. I have thoroughly scanned the new *Catechism of the Catholic Church* with this possibility in mind. There is no denying that in some passages the changeover to a genuine ethic of responsibility is achieved or at least suggested. But on a large number of points the *Catechism* still formulates a morality exclusively for subjects. It speaks to those "who are under the law and authority," but scarcely mentions those who hold authority in the Church.

One characteristic example of this is the so-called Sunday obligation. The *Catechism* teaches categorically that every single
deliberate missing of Mass on Sundays and holy days of obligation is "a serious sin" (*CCC* 2181). By contrast, the question isn't
even raised as to what sins the highest authorities in the Church
may commit, for instance, by absolutely insisting on the linkage
of ordination with celibacy. But it is that choice which makes it
impossible for many parishes and individual Christians to celebrate the Eucharist regularly because there are too few priests.
For this legal reason, thousands of Catholic parishes are not real
eucharistic communities, although they would like to be. What
are the consequences of this for Christian life?

In his encyclical *Veritatis Splendor,* Pope John Paul II shows a
complete lack of understanding for teleologically based natural
theology, which is one of the key features of an ethic of responsibility. It is clear, of course, that any predominantly teleological
moral theology escapes most external controls. By contrast, a
purely deontological morality, which also emphasizes the universal, identical, and historically unchangeable demands of the so-
called natural law, is well suited for control by church authority.

7

The Changeover in Moral Theology and the Crisis of the Sacrament of Penance

The crisis of the sacrament of penance—everywhere lamented in the Church—has nothing, or not much, to do with the changeover and new directions in moral theology. Needless to say, moral theology after Vatican II is no longer a "morality of the confessional." It is a morality of life, which can get a great deal of impetus from the sacrament of reconciliation and *shalom*. But the way to this is not through standardized control.

In my experience, one reason why the crisis of the sacrament of penance intensified was the fact that the old pastoral approach to confession went too far. I have heard many hundreds of confessions in which penitents told me that they hadn't been to confession for years. Why? Because they had been forbidden absolution on account of the so-called sin of "marital onanism." Thanks especially to the influence of Saint Alphonsus Liguori, for almost two centuries wise confessors hadn't asked about coitus interruptus.

The encyclical *Casti Connubii* (1930), however, categorically demanded this sort of checking up. Married couples were bidden to accept children "as they came." Most penitents who already had a large family rejected this idea. But that left them with a decision to make.

The first "solution" was to promise to obey the encyclical while knowing that the promise would never be kept. That way at least one got absolution. The second possibility was honestly to tell the confessor that one didn't want anymore children; in which case, "obedient" confessors, though their hearts may have bled, would refuse absolution. A sizeable group opted for a third solution: stop going to confession until menopause. In most cases, this also meant not taking communion.

Here it becomes obvious how little consideration the old moral theology gave to the historical dimension of behavior. Confessors could stand by the Augustinian position that every conjugal act must be oriented to procreation, that is, unless, like Alphonsus Liguori, they had the courage to challenge this thesis and leave the matter to the conscience of the married couple.

Actually, up to a point, clinging to Augustine's rule might have made sense: almost as late as our own day the human race needed a maximum number of births to guarantee its survival. Today, by contrast, the situation is reversed. On an ecologically threatened, planet humanity needs far-reaching birth control or contraception for the sake of its own survival. Then, too, modern theology and anthropology have both recognized that Augustine's statement is false. Every marital act should promote love, unity, and fidelity. Very few acts of intercourse can and should aim at procreation.

But this example is only one factor, though of course a typical one, in explaining how an exaggerated and senseless pastoral control over penance worked. It drove people away from the sacrament of reconciliation, thereby creating today's crisis of the sacrament of penance.

Then another historical development occurred. In the course

of polemics with the Protestants, the "administration" (a dreadful term, but it was used) of penance took on a brand-new, historically determined form. It reflected the whole self-concept of the Church that came about after the Reformation. With increasing one-sidedness, western theology saw in the "father confessor" the *judge*. He was the man who had to know the exact nature and number of the serious sins committed, in order to impose the right penance and to be able to forgive sins. Thus confession became a particularly vivid symbol of a judging and controlling Church.

If anything good managed to come out of such a pastoral atmosphere, we basically have Saint Alphonsus Liguori to thank. He was brave enough to adopt, by and large, the approach of the Eastern Churches to the sacrament of healing and reconciliation. In these Churches, a clear distinction was almost always made between the institution of public confession, on the one hand, and the celebration of the healing praise of God's compassion on the other.

From this fruitful viewpoint, Alphonsus describes, with many variations, the role of the confessor as follows: he should be, above all, a mirror of the compassion of the heavenly Father, and thus lead the way to fulfilling the target commandment: "Be merciful as your heavenly Father is merciful." He is to be an impressive image of Christ, the Divine Physician, and connect healing love with the preaching of reconciliation. Only then does the role of "judge" emerge, but it has to be understood as the cultivation of the gift of discernment and guiding the way to its acquisition. Seen from this angle, the confessor is to encourage penitents to look on their whole life in the light of the commandment to love one another.

The crisis of the sacrament of penance will be overcome nowadays only to the extent that everyone can see and sense in the Church's view of itself and its moral preaching the example and the norm of the Servant of God, humble and ready to suffer. The

Church must manifest the One who teaches us the healing, non-violent, and powerful love that puts an end to hatred through his example, his word, and his grace.

From this standpoint, the sacrament of the messianic *shalom*, of reconciliation, peace and salvation can and will have to take on a new form. Then the celebrations by the group and the individual will be able to complete each other. But the sacrament in all its forms must always express the dynamic of the seventh Beatitude: "Blessed are the peacemakers, for they shall be called sons and daughters of God." In other words, "Blessed are the nonviolent," who with their healing love turn enemies into friends.

The post-Tridentine practice of the sacrament of penance was symptomatic of the way the Church understood itself, with all its structures, and indicative of the Roman brand of morality. This practice undoubtedly had its dark side, a fact that becomes evidence in the examples cited previously.

This practice also fostered an explosion of scrupulosity that was unique in the history of Christianity. In order to be certain of forgiveness and salvation, one had to confess all serious sins, their number and nature, along with any circumstances that might alter the case. Handbooks of moral theology had such a long and complicated catalogue of transgressions that anxious penitents, especially in the hands of an unskillful confessor, could never decide whether they had really confessed all their sins.

The new *Catechism of the Catholic Church* still has quite an extensive list of serious sins. That is in keeping with the will of the pope, who insists on a complete rundown of everything that must be believed or viewed as a moral duty. To be sure, the *Catechism* is not so excessive on this score as the older handbooks of moral theology were. It also clearly notes that over the course of history there has been a wide variety in the notions and forms of the sacrament of penance (*CCC* 1447).

Even though the *Catechism* offers no clear guidelines for re-solving the crisis in the sacrament of penance, there *are* some new tones and perspectives articulated. The sacrament of pen-ance is treated under the heading of "the sacrament of healing," alongside the anointing of the sick (*CCC* 1421). "Confession" is interpreted from the standpoint of praising the holiness and mercy of God (*CCC* 1442), which moves in the direction of the Eastern Churches. There is as yet no concrete statement about the new form of penance, though one finds the first steps headed that way.

In my opinion, one long-lasting and widespread Western prac-tice from the Middle Ages might be helpful: several times a year general absolution used to be given by bishops, abbots, and so on, in a community penitential celebration. But this was under the condition that "serious sins" were confessed individually. The decisive feature of this model is the explanation of what serious sins were: *et quidem criminalia*, which meant sins that are also crimes. These were described precisely, so that there were no need-lessly tormenting scruples about what had to be confessed.

An up-to-date pastoral approach to penance that made use of this old practice would be a good thing. It could connect group celebration with a strong accent on solidarity in salvation and on the worst sins against it. It could link personal confession as praise for God's mercy with a continually reinforced obligation to peace, reconciliation, healing love, and justice. That would also be a major step toward both ecumenical reconciliation with the Orthodox Church and an approximation to the viewpoint of the Reformed Churches; and it would set the agenda for inculturation in the here and now.

8

Christian Ethics
in Ecumenical Dialogue

One of the most obvious weak points of Catholic ecumenism since the Council lies in the lack of dialogue about ticklish problems in moral theology. This is extremely significant because, in my opinion, the ecumenical changeover, the ecumenical turnaround and new directions in moral theology for the Catholic Church are all bound up together in many different ways. Limiting ecumenical dialogue to purely "dogmatic" issues would be a big step backward, because the breathtaking, fortunate ecumenical changeover is closely tied to the changeover in moral theology. And both changes are bound up with the question of the structures and self-concept of the Catholic Church.

The schisms between Rome and the Byzantine Catholic Churches of the East, like the splits that occurred in the wake of the Reformation, were reflected and hardened in the Roman Catholic Church by a completely new type of moral theology that would have been unimaginable anywhere else. Take, for example, the matters of synodal structure, sacramental spirituality, the preeminence of pneumatology in the whole understanding of life, the therapeutic perspective of *oikonomia* (God's attitude of housefather/housemother, mirrored in dealings with the law) in the Eastern Churches, or the Pauline stress on feeling in the Reformed approach to Christian ethics: all those who supported such things inevitably viewed the legalism, centralism, and interlocking controls of Catholic moral theology as an insuperable hurdle to reconciliation, much less reunion.

I was overjoyed one day when an Anglican archbishop in *The London Times* voiced his conviction that my work as a moral theologian had largely removed this hurdle. Of course, it would be naive to ascribe such a turnaround to me personally. It was the *kairós*, the salvific opportunity of the moment, that sent many important theologians, in exegesis, dogmatic theology, and Christian ethics, on a quest for a renewal that would serve the basic concern of ecumenism. In my mind—but I certainly wasn't the only one—this concern came first and foremost.

In the German-speaking world moral theology found models and incentives in some of its great nineteenth-century theologians, above all, Johann Michael Sailer, Johann Baptist Hirscher (a moral theologian from Freising), Magnus Jocham (who built bridges to the Eastern Churches through his sacramental perspective), and Franz Xavier Linsenmann. (Linsenmann was a great Tübingen professor from the second half of the nineteenth century, who proved that the Pauline model of the grace-filled pathos of freedom could find a home in the Catholic Church as well.)

In this context, the meaning of the Second Vatican Council both for the ecumenical movement and for the renewal and turnaround in moral theology can't be rated highly enough. Beyond what has already been said, I would point to the elaboration of the doctrine of the adult Christian in the Church. The overcoming of clericalism (by no means complete) is extremely important for the life of all the Churches and their reconciliation. It is significant as well as for the elaboration of a moral theology that is fruitful by the standards of salvation history.

The Situation After the Council

The Council sparked a powerful dynamism in theology, including moral theology. In Germany, the legacy of the great nineteenth-century moral theologians could now finally be "received" and propagated. An ecumenical collaboration that could have scarcely been imagined before now began to take shape. Even during the Council, I received invitations for guest professorships at some of the most important Protestant theological faculties in the United States. Let me mention only Union Theological Seminary at Columbia University in New York and Yale Divinity School.

After the conclusion of my stay at Yale, I was offered a chair for Catholic moral theology with an emphasis on ecumenism. The position was eventually accepted by a nun, Sister Margaret Farley, who like so many other Catholic theologians had taken her doctorate with Protestant Professor James Gustafson. As a bridge-builder for a true ecumenical Christian ethics, Gustafson has made an extraordinary contribution.

In Germany, important works in moral theology were soon being produced through ecumenical collaboration, for example, the three-volume work *The Authority of Freedom: The Present and Future of the Council*[7] by Protestant conciliar observer Johann Christoph Hampe. Another three-volume work, *Manual of Christian Ethics*, by Anselm Herz, Wilhelm Korff, Trutz Rendtorff, and Hermann Ringeling, illuminates more than practically any other work the enormous progress that has been made.

Protestant theologian Wolfgang Nethöfel evaluates postconciliar ecumenical achievements in his book *Moral Theology After the Council: Persons, Programs, Positions.*[8] Well-informed, unbiased, elegant in manner, he clearly shows that the age of sterile, disputatious theology is past. The convergences exceed the differences.

We are living in a fruitful learning community, amid reconciled diversity and astonishing relatedness.

What *Gaudium et Spes* said about the solidarity of Christians with all human beings who are striving for truth and responsibility is especially true for ecumenical collaboration in the domain of Christian ethics: "Through loyalty to conscience Christians are joined to other men in the search for truth and for the right solution to so many moral problems which arise both in the life of individuals and from social relationships" (*GS* 16).

Catholic and Protestant moral theologians are joyfully aware today that we are bound by more than just the moral law inscribed in the hearts of all men and women. We are obliged still more by common faith in Christ and his Gospel to join in the search for a constantly deeper and historically more valid knowledge of the "law of the Spirit of life in Christ Jesus."

Here Catholic moral theologians differ from Protestant ethicists by their readiness to listen to the Church's magisterium. But both know they are rooted in the religious sense of the people of God, and both value ecumenical dialogue between church leaders.

The Gulf Between Theology and the Hierarchy

Since the Second Vatican Council, a productive dialogue has started up between representatives of the leadership in the various Churches on almost all basic doctrinal questions related to Christian unity. In these discussion groups, highly qualified theologians have had their say. The program of dialogue has proved difficult on the question of church offices and structures, but there, too, we can see progress.

Very delicate problems, by contrast, emerge in ecumenical dialogue on all the issues involving moral theology. In fact, within the Catholic Church—above all, between the supreme magisterium and professional theologians—this same point has caused and continues to cause serious tension.

The hottest arguments have swirled around sexual morality, particularly contraception and the pastoral care of divorced people. There is no lack of excellent monographs that address these problems in their ecumenical dimensions and thereby, as I and many others hope, lay promising groundwork for future official dialogue. In each case, we have to become thoroughly familiar with old and new, convergent and divergent views. But on these very questions there is, at times, a seemingly insuperable gap between church leaders on one side and the theologians and large groups of believers on the other.

The Ecumenical Explosiveness of the Birth Control Question

One of the most respected English moral theologians, Kevin I. Kelly, has written a model book about the problem of Catholic-Anglican dialogue on bioethical issues: *Life and Love: Towards a Christian Dialogue on Bioethical Questions*.[9] Apart from its high scholarly quality, the book is interesting because, in England, official Catholic-Anglican dialogue has now taken up the same questions raised by Kelly.

Like the Reformed Churches in general, the Anglican Church had dragged along with it the burden of Augustinian rigorism. Anglicans, like Catholics, had long hesitated between the strict Augustinian position (marital intercourse is morally good only when it aims at procreation) and the toleration of pragmatic pastoral approaches such as Alphonsus Liguori's.

After years of dispute, in 1929 the Lambeth Conference officially decided that contraception was a morally acceptable compromise solution, provided some essential criteria were met. This is worth noting as far as ecumenical dialogue goes, because a year later there were harsh reprisals from Rome. Pius XI felt he had to confront the Anglican community and similar efforts in other Reformed Churches; so insisted on the strict Augustinian party line. His encyclical *Casti Connubii* explicitly labeled contraception a crime ("and abortion is another crime").

By a wide majority, the commission that Pope Paul VI set up to deal with population issues voted to revise *Casti Connubii*. But the spokesmen for the minority felt it was unthinkable that the Holy Spirit might be working more effectively with the Anglicans at the Lambeth Conference than with the pope of Rome. This peculiar attitude shows how difficult a transition it was and is (especially for church officials) from a theology of controversy to interconfessional dialogue and willingness to learn from others.

Kevin Kelly makes it clear how much ecumenical dialogue between scholars differs from official dialogue. A crucial problem comes up when, on the Catholic side, only Rome's official pronouncements get to be heard, not the views of the overwhelming majority of Catholic scholars. This dilemma has to be seen in all its sharpness: how will sister Churches engaged in official dialogue react when they see either no one but conformists representing the Catholic Church or high-level spokesmen just rubber-stamping Rome's views without any personal conviction?

The unofficial dialogue continues, while within the Catholic Church the exchange between the Vatican and the theologians has stagnated. There is a serious difficulty here: the "reception" of papal teachings by the "people of God," and more specifically by experts in theology and the social sciences. On the other hand, we have to ask about the papal "reception" of the findings of theology, including the work of ecumenists.

One point must be noted: there can be no genuine "reception" of the ecumenical new departure, indeed the full-scale ecumenical conversion, that took place in Vatican II without at least taking seriously the standpoint of the Orthodox and Reformed sister Churches on such vital issues. And their views have to be incorporated into conversation between the Churches. Sincere dialogue within the Church and ecumenical dialogue outside it belong inseparably together.

Indissolubility of Marriage and Pastoral Care for the Divorced

Ecumenical dialogue is especially complicated on the question of the indissolubility of marriage and the pastoral care of divorced persons, whose numbers are distressingly high—and apparently still rising—due to the enormous cultural changes of recent years. Here, too, ecumenical dialogue is particularly urgent, given the many mixed marriages.

Pioneering work in this area has taken place in discussions between the Orthodox Churches in the United States and the American Catholic Bishops Conference. This is a model of an ecumenical community willing to learn in common service to salvation and the healing of all those involved.

A priceless service for the dialogue hoped for on this issue has been rendered by the thorough study of Gabriele Lachner, *The Churches and the Remarriage of Divorced Persons*.[10] The situation in the Catholic Church has been accurately described by Yale moral theologian Margaret Farley in *Divorce, Remarriage and Pastoral Practice*.[11] She comes to the conclusion: "The past twenty-five years have seen important changes in the Roman Catholic Church with regard to divorce and remarriage. These changes are clearly shown in the writings of moral theologians, in the practice of marriage courts, and in the viewpoint and judgments of a growing number of persons, who consider themselves loyal members of the Catholic Church. The affirmation of the changes among theologians is not unanimous, but it is widespread enough to be reliably characterized as the attitude of a clear majority" (p. 213).

At the Würzburg Synod of the West German dioceses, as at the Roman Bishops Synod of 1980, which produced the apostolic letter *Familiaris Consortio*, the pope was given an urgent request. He was asked to see if the Catholic Church might not borrow some features from the consistent practice of the Orthodox Churches with regard to the pastoral care of the divorced.

Thanks to the new ecumenical departures and the collaboration of theologians from all Churches, thanks to a coming together and a sharing by all parts of the still-divided Christian world, everyone is better capable of knowing God's will on this painful question. The three highly respected bishops from the Upper Rhine—Karl Lehmann, Oskar Saier, and Walter Kasper—have carefully pointed to viable approaches to this problem in their book *On Pastoral Accompaniment of People From Broken Marriages, Divorced, Separated, and Remarried Persons.*

The most important points to be considered both for ecumenical dialogue and for future pastoral care are the following: in sacred Scripture, the accent on questions of conjugal morals lies not on banning marriage for the divorced but on banning separation. This requires that everything humanly possible be done to make marriages succeed and last.

The Bible and the whole of Christian tradition point to accessible paths for the pastoral care of the divorced. Of course, these require a highly developed gift of discernment. The critical feature here, in my opinion, is that ever since the Council, even in the Roman Catholic Church, marriage is no longer regarded as a contract, but as a sacramental alliance. If the marriage contract as such were the sacrament, then after divorce it could still hang like a sword over the head of all those involved.

Suppose, by contrast, marriage should be looked on as a bond of life and a sacrament of salvation. Then we could no longer demand that couples persist in the bond of matrimony once it was definitely clear that a concrete marriage not only wasn't serving the spiritual welfare and healthy human relations of the couple, but was actually destroying them. Paul's dictum still holds true, "It is to peace that God has called you" (1 Cor 7:15).

These extremely painful and pressing problems show us how much the process of reconciliation within the Church, patient dialogue, and the breaking down of mistrust is demanded by the ecumenical changeover, and how much these same processes will be made possible by it. If carried out seriously and humbly, ecumenical dialogue can contribute a great deal to peace within the Church, The unavoidable tensions have to endured with Christian patience.[12]

It is my firm conviction that the ecumenical changeover throughout the Christian world constitutes a single grand call by God to grace. No part of a separate Christendom can be inwardly healed to any great degree without fidelity to the ecumenical new departure, without decisively demonstrating ecumenical readiness to learn and undergo conversion, and without steady perseverance in ecumenical efforts. This calls for not just wisdom, but much patience and an advance of mutual trust.

The Church's understanding of itself, including its structures, and the constant effort to renew and deepen moral theology will flourish best if we keep our eyes on our ecumenical calling. Hence I believe that in the face of all the crises the Church is going through, we have to start here at this point and stay with it.

9

Continuous Inculturation

One of the most delicate topics in the Roman Catholic Church is that of inculturation, the rooting of Christian faith in different cultural spaces. The other Christian Churches in the Western world are likewise having a difficult time with this problem. Here I give one example in lieu of many: in Africa, where dance is half of life, Baptist missionaries emphatically forbid dancing.

This dimension of renewal made its way into my own thinking after I read a review of my book *The Law of Christ* by the well-known missiologist Thomas Ohm. After some exaggerated praise, he warned that this book was "still far too Eurocentric." That review was a wake-up call for me, and I began to ask myself questions. My dealings with my colleagues, friends, and students from all over the world heightened my impression that fidelity to Christ's charge to evangelize all nations made it necessary to do some serious rethinking.

Great efforts had to be made so that faith in Christ, the savior of the whole world, could be rooted in every human heart and every culture. I was helped by directing a whole series of doctoral theses on this subject by highly gifted students from different parts of the globe. How far, I wondered, should I back their courageous attempts toward rooting Christian morality in their culture, and where did I have to warn them to exercise restraint?

Inculturation in Rome and in the "Latin Church"

We have the grace accorded Paul, the Apostle of the Gentiles, to thank for the fact that the Good News managed to spread throughout the Roman Empire, with some help from the language of koine Greek. The great patriarchates of Jerusalem, Antioch, and Alexandria allowed, as a matter of course, the evolution of an independent Roman patriarchate, which even included a "Roman rite."

There was no centralism to prevent the Gospel from sending down roots in the most varied cultures and language groups. On a number of issues the African Church, with its center in Carthage, took different paths from the Church in Rome. Due to successful inculturation, the spread of Christianity in England proceeded apace, expanding out from there, as many Germanic tribes on the Continent accepted the Gospel. In marital law, Germanic tradition soon prevailed, through a kind of synthesis with Roman law.

The work of the missions would have been unthinkable, if everything back then had been spelled out as precisely as it now is in the "Latin Church." If the Church of Rome would nowadays grant the Churches in Africa, Asia, and Latin America the same degree of autonomy that the oldest Eastern patriarchates gave Rome as a matter of course in the early days, then the track would be cleared for the Gospel.

Objectively speaking, the Vatican has not only made foolish mistakes on the subject of inculturation; it has out and out sinned by a monstrous excess of regulation. This is most obvious in the way it stifled the hopeful mission in China through its harsh imposition of the Latin rite, Roman canon law, and European theology.

In my opinion, there can be no full and fruitful turnaround on this basic issue without a humble backing off from every kind of triumphalism. Only a very humble Church, a humble theology, and a radical departure from centralized systems of control can dismantle the impediments to genuine inculturation.

More Than Mere Accommodation

Ever since the middle of the twentieth century, critical voices have been increasingly raised against needless alienation in preaching the Gospel to, for example, Africa and Asia. They have loudly insisted on the duty to make adaptations on acute individual issues, such as the veneration of ancestors, liturgical colors and vestments, and, more cautiously, canon law. As the Roman Synod for Africa has made perfectly clear, we have moved far beyond this first phase. The question is no longer whether to make a few cosmetic adjustments, but of faith's becoming *rooted* in other cultures.

The two crucial points of departure for a successful process of establishing roots are, first, a profound realization of the simplicity of biblical thinking, above all of the Gospels. The whole freight of scholastic philosophy and theology, and even of successful, more or less inculturated contemporary European or North American theology, has to be set aside. The second prerequisite is a loving and thorough knowledge of each individual nation, intimacy with the thinking and feeling of the people, along with respect for other cultures.

The Right to Make Mistakes

The full rooting of the Gospel in a concrete culture and tradition is a difficult and sometimes long process. Anyone who thinks it has to be controlled in advance and channeled from the outside has already made a crucial mistake.

Full rooting takes place step by step and calls for a respectful dialogue within the local church of the same kind that is now being developed in the common ground between the different Eastern Churches and, of course, Rome. One has to have the courage to proceed without anxiously anticipating mistakes, confident that mistakes are meant to be corrected.

But some mistakes can be spotted early on and so are absolutely to be avoided, like sending out missionaries or bishops saddled with a cultural superiority complex. This can easily lead to the notion that along with the Gospel one has to bring one's "higher" culture. We shouldn't let ourselves be deceived: even if that culture *were* higher and better, the result of the work of such apostles will always be cultural infiltration and proselytizing.

A similar mistake is made when a missionary arrives loaded down with a theology framed by his own culture and tradition. Still worse, such men sometimes think that they have to recite the whole catalogue of doctrines that the Church of their origins has multiplied, sometimes astronomically, on matters of faith and morals.

One has to be fully aware of the grace and burden of any given theology. Then, upon moving into a different cultural context, one won't begin by proclaiming and imposing marginal doctrines and commandments. With inculturation, you must always aim, first and foremost, at the center: at the belief that God the Father has glorified his humble Servant and Son Jesus and granted the gifts of the Holy Spirit to those who believe in him with all their heart.

The medium for this sort of well-rooted preaching is a biblical kind of narrative theology. We cannot and should not begin with a systematic exposition of doctrines that one way or another must sound alien. First, we must simply relate God's saving deeds, as the New Testament teaches us. Paul himself teaches the basics of inculturation by example. He strove tirelessly to be all things to all people, to be a Jew to the Jews, a brother to both Greeks and non-Greeks.

The second point about inculturation that we could learn from Paul and the whole apostolic Church is to aim to have the native peoples of an area take over the services and offices of the Church as quickly as possible. For this, as we see in the primitive Church, they must be given a great advance of trust; and we must remain in brotherly-sisterly dialogue with them.

Meaning of the Social Sciences

As I have already pointed out, Professor Ohm's hint that my overview of moral theology was still flawed by Eurocentrism threw me into a sort of terror. With increased dedication I took systematic counsel of the social sciences, that is, the sociology of knowledge, sociological studies of cultures and customs, more specifically of sexuality, marriage, and the family, and, not least, of types of power and forms of religious organization.

Thorough familiarity with these and related fields makes one extremely cautious about any kind of generalization. It inoculates one against the mania of believing that in any single culture one has an eternal, complete and unchangeable body of knowledge, as if it were some kind of law of nature regulating everything.

Coping With the Present and the Future, Reappraising the Past

In order to acquire and transmit competence in matters of inculturation, it is not enough to study "horizontally," for example, the various governance systems of the various Churches. Above all, it is important to understand what sort of relationship exists between concurrent family and political structures and the modes of church governance as they have taken form, changed, or become solidified.

The whole history of the shapes and kinds of moralities, customs, and moral philosophies has to be studied carefully. We have to look at all their reciprocal connections with the world of today, and discover what the sociology of the various sorts of power and morality have to tell us—a good deal I might imagine. A historical overview of the sociology of canon law in the different Churches would be useful for the purposes of inculturation. But first we have to investigate the interaction between modes of power in the family, society, and the state and the evolution of successful, unsuccessful, or wasted opportunities for the reform of canon law.

Inculturation: More Than a Matter for Missionary Churches

Every part of the Christian world, most especially the Church of Rome—considering its enormous influence—must face the issue of inculturation with an view to its own "genuine" cultural milieu. Every part of the Church bears, consciously or otherwise, an enormous burden of more or less successful inculturations, of used and unused opportunities for inculturation in the past. Still more, the whole texture and every dimension of the Church as it actually exists call for fundamental revision in keeping with the extent and nature of cultural and other changes.

Our contemporary world is marked by an unprecedented speeding-up of historical change. All of us live, in one way or another, in a simultaneous nonsimultaneity, that is, we are at once in and out of touch with other people with whom we share out planet. Every individual lives that disjunction in himself or herself, either as a productive tension and opportunity or as a cause of multifarious blockages.

We also experience this tension-filled state of being in touch and out of touch in our relationships within the Church. The artistic and cultural avant-garde and the lively new generation are tuned to different wavelengths, for example, than tradition-bound individuals and groups. The latter have grown up with the old Roman morality and they try to find security in it. Realizing this and creatively organizing that tension is a great challenge and an indispensable key to the solution of the present crisis in the Church.

Inculturation and the History of Moral Theology

The whole history of moral theology, in fact, must be reviewed from the standpoint of inculturation with all its variants in the different epochs and regions of the Church. We have to ask the question: Why it was neglected or frustrated in some eras?

Special attention has to be paid to successful forms of the inculturation of morality as part of the larger process of inculturating the Gospel. And ecumenical dialogue on moral theology will likewise be helped by a better understanding of inculturation. That includes both successful, less successful, and unacceptable forms and modes of conscious and unconscious inculturation in the various Churches and parts of the world.

We absolutely cannot understand inculturation without scrutinizing the different interactions between the structures of belief and morality and the forms of rule in family and society, between the prevailing elites and their influence on the Church. In this perspective, for example, an important question arises: who were the preferred addressees of the Gospel in certain contexts? Who got the most attention and respect? The powerful, the successful, the strong and the healthy, or also, and quite specifically, the poor, the oppressed, and the marginalized? Did people really follow Jesus' example here? A clear awareness of these problems serves to shield us from the dangers of fanaticism and oversimplification.

A Cautionary Example

Why did the Church lose a majority of its workers in the nineteenth and the early twentieth century? Because the workers were never even considered in crucial areas of the Church's life, structures, and forms of rule. Why did so many religiously gifted women leave the convent (as they still continue to do so to this day)? A thorough analysis of yesterday's and today's forms of inculturation can point to the direction in which answers and solutions at least can begin to be discovered. Along with the issue of women's rights, we are increasingly troubled by the question: Will we win or lose the young people, the new generation?

This brief outline may show how great a mistake it is to assume that a new inculturation is needed only in Africa and Latin America.

10

Today's Burning Issues

In studying the latest encyclical on morality *Veritatis Splendor* and the new *Catechism of the Catholic Church*, I have mainly asked myself: How do they treat today's most vexing issues? And do they ask the questions being raised by the social, cultural, and religious elites?

There may be some argument about what these questions are in particular, but I am convinced, along with many of the most active participants in ecumenical dialogue, that the following problem areas need to be examined: *peace* in all its dimensions, especially those of healing nonviolence and reconciling love; *worldwide justice* as an end in itself and as a path to peace; global and urgent *responsibility for our endangered planet*, and the ecological norms and virtues that this danger has made a necessity. Was any *joint effort* made before putting the new *Catechism of the Catholic Church* together to examine the signs of the times in the light of the pastoral constitution *Gaudium et Spes*? Did anyone look first for the encouraging and challenging signs, and only then look for the threatening ones? The answer, unfortunately, is all too obvious.

Next comes the examination of conscience for moral theologians: Have we done our spadework? Have we articulated the situation properly? I don't think we have any reasons for self-congratulation. On the other hand, we *have* made some progress on these and

similar issues—enough to draw upon us aversion and anger, or at
least a good deal of mistrust.

Nowadays I think that our approach hasn't been sufficiently
therapeutic. Above all, we have done too little to bring the crucial
phenomenon of simultaneous nonsimultaneity, of belonging and not
belonging, to the attention of the contemporary world. We have let
ourselves get sidetracked and have fought over secondary issues.

An Ethics of Peace

René Girard, Raymund Schwager, and many others have pointed
to the centrality of violence and nonviolence in the total picture
of human history, especially in our time. The key to the great
drama of redemption that we celebrate, proclaim, and try to live
out is the healing nonviolence and reconciling love of the Redeemer of the world.

The Christian doctrine of redemption is not about washing away
"the stain of original sin" from the souls of children, but saving the
world as a whole from the disastrous chain of violence and counter-
violence. Jesus emphatically lives his calling with an eye to the four
Suffering Servant songs of Second Isaiah. He reveals, above all, on
the cross and in the Resurrection, the saving path of healing, reconciling love, and active, creative nonviolence. These things would have
to take a crucial position in any renewed moral theology. And all
this must be inculturated into the here and now; it has to be
preached in an up-to-date fashion and made a palpable presence.

Do we neglect to create enthusiastic and decisive core groups
for the nonviolent solution of conflicts, and then never even bring
the matter up for discussion in moral theology? If so, we have
been sidetracked, and we are getting others sidetracked as well.

Whoever can, right here, right now, convincingly and stirringly
illuminate individual consciousness and community life in this

light and this dynamic of healing nonviolence and reconciling love is on the way to true simultaneity and inculturation. Such persons are, in the best sense, contemporaries of Christ. At the same time they are, even though in a different sense, but with the same dynamic, contemporaries of today's humanity which is so threatened by violence and in particular of all those who show the way by word and example.

Mere admonitions to peace are surely not enough in our shaken time. We need strong and living faith in Christ, the suffering Servant of God. We need a radical decision to follow him on the path of peace, as he proclaimed it and attested to it in living, dying, and rising. This is part of the framework both of the teaching of faith and of Christian morals. The Second Vatican Council has set up guidelines here; but it did not, of course, fully develop the meaning of what it pointed out. Still, Christian movements such as Pax Christi offer hope for the future, above all, if a renewed moral theology joins them in moving ahead wholeheartedly on this path.

Worldwide Efforts for Justice in All Its Dimensions

The Church has adopted the agenda of human rights, an agenda which was first raised in the secular world. It did so, of course, with some hesitation; though it has happily gone on to promote them—in some areas at least. Still, there is a lot more consciousness-raising to be done.

If we want inner and outer peace, then we have to join hands and help to decrease the slope between the North and the South. It is a crime that cries to heaven, a crime against the Creator and all of humanity, when a bare fifth of the human race, namely the inhabitants of the Northern Hemisphere, seize four-fifths of the most valuable raw materials and then spew out nearly four-fifths of the pollution on our planet and destroy its ecological balance.

There is more at stake here than justice between the former colonial powers and their old exploited territories. There is also the wrong being done, and our responsibility, to future generations. The wasting of the most important resources and the disturbance or destruction of our planet's ecological balance are likewise a grave injustice in this global sense.

What Is Happening With Life on Our Planet?

For the first time in our long history, human beings have the power to extinguish all life. They could do this at a stroke with their stockpile of nuclear weapons, or slowly through the destruction of the ecological foundations of life. This situation calls for a radical rethinking. Concern with artificial contraception seems to repress this life-threatening crisis. Of course, the problem of overpopulation will not be solved by the massive distribution of contraceptives. But this whole complex of problems has to be clearly addressed, and responsible solutions have to be pointed out or at least adequately discussed and jointly sought for.

We know from the animal world that a huge increase in any given population can lead to unimaginable explosions of violence. And we are familiar with the fact that the human population explosion, along with global migration, has skyrocketed the crime rate and the inclination to violence. No responsible ethics of peace or ecological ethics can fail to confront these problems. In fact, they must be moved into the conscious center of applied morality.

The ecumenical gathering in Basel and then the worldwide version in Seoul were first steps in this direction. The leadership of the Catholic Church took them only with hesitation. This, too, proves that the turnaround in moral theology has not yet won the day. This isn't the place to address these issues in depth. I have tried to do that in my other publications.

11

The Turnaround From Moral Individualism to Solidarity in Salvation

This chapter addresses areas of moral theology that are very close to our personal and historical skin. They can be dealt with only if we develop a new perspective and a new kind of intelligence. They demand a radical rethinking in the direction of comprehensive, even cosmic solidarity.

In this case, moral theology as an individual discipline is facing too many demands and, for this very reason, it may not limit itself to moral "oughts." Its power, after all, comes from faith. Hence at the crucial points, where further reflection cannot be put off, what we must have is the grand overview that motivates and orients people.

Part of the problem, in my mind, is the way we understand the conceptual pair *original sin-redemption*. The discussions on that subject in the new *Catechism of the Catholic Church* strike me as not very helpful. They seem to presuppose that the biblical stories of Adam have to be believed as historical facts, down to the details. Thus, for example, the *Catechism* says that if Adam and Eve had not sinned in Paradise, human beings would have been spared *physical death*.

Yet the Bible's statements about original sin tell us a great deal in the context of belief in redemption in Christ. Adam is not a historical personality who can be assigned a date. He is the embodiment of the entire human race's solidarity in salvation. This idea is not based on *monogenism* (the descent of all human beings from a single couple), but, much more deeply and radically, on *monotheism*.

God, the Creator, is one in three persons. What he creates, coming from this source, stands steadfast in a profound, comprehensive solidarity, first willed in the good. Yet if this solidarity is rejected, the person does not land on his own feet; he stigmatizes himself into solidarity with disaster. As for this state—whatever we call it—we can as Christians think and speak of it only in the light of faith in redemption. That redemption in turn is marked by an unsurpassably dense web of solidarity uniting all people in the good, in Christ. Our union is so deep and wide that we little human beings can never completely exhaust it even in the light of faith. The whole of moral theology must bear the stamp of this mystery.

If that is the case, then Christian conversion can no longer be narrowed into an individualistic or legalistic bind. Its own center of gravity leads it to think and act in solidarity on all the issues we have already addressed. That includes the common struggle for liberating and healing nonviolence, for peace in all dimensions, and worldwide justice. A global sense of responsibility, prompted by current findings on the fate of our planet and on our common ecological tasks, has to enter people's consciousness. As soon as it does, it confronts us with a basic decision: either for the salvation of everyone or involvement in a bottomless and boundless solidarity in disaster.

The doctrine of original sin and redemption, rightly understood, leads by its own inner logic to an understanding of the human and ethical "basic option." This basic option does have to be carried out personally; but still it must be understood in a radically communitarian way, in keeping with its contents and dynamic.

That is what I and, no doubt, most theologians who have seriously considered the issue of the "basic option" were and are concerned with. The latter has nothing to do, as *Veritatis Splendor* seems to insist, with watering down the concept of sin. Much less does it sweep away, for all practical purposes, the doctrine of mortal sin.

The basic option, as we see it, is radical; it is a fundamental orientation that must be deeply rooted in the heart, will, and character of a person. Of course, it can also help us with the question that vexed the old manuals of moral theology: how can I know whether I have committed a mortal sin (which I then absolutely have to confess)? Our view is no superficial attempt to tranquilize people's minds. But it *can* liberate them from needless scrupulosity without endangering a person's good basic orientation.

Presupposing all this, what happens when we meet men and women of good will, who really wish to live by faith and with their eyes on the Kingdom of God, but who, despite their good will, sometimes fail on some concrete point? We can say to them something like this: if, after you fail and despite your failure in one area, the good basic orientation of your mind and energy and actions is intact, then you can be sure that you have remained in God's grace. This statement and the view behind it does not allow for any sort of cheap excuses. On the contrary, this view helps strengthen the roots of the basic orientation to the good and its fruitfulness.

It is important to me in this context not to misunderstand the basic option in an individualistic sense, as in the phrase "I want to save my soul." Instead, I mean a profound, comprehensive decision for salvific solidarity in Christ. Scripture says on this point: "Bear one another's burdens, and in this way you will fulfill the law of Christ" (Gal 6:2); or, as we just now said apropos of the great responsibilities of our historical moment: we need decisive commitment to healing and liberating nonviolence, for peace in all dimensions, for comprehensive justice and ecological responsibility, and, in the domain of faith, radical commitment to the ecumene.

We receive our freedom in Christ through his all-embracing salvific solidarity. It is not a gift to be selfishly walked off with, but a gift *and* an assignment to work for freedom and the salvation of all people, insofar as that lies in our power.

The many controversial points in *Veritatis Splendor* derive from its characteristically post-Tridentine concentration on a mere morality of the act. The leading emphasis of this sort of moral doctrine is on listing intrinsically, absolutely evil actions, which admit of no exceptions and are binding under pain of mortal sin. Sins against the sixth commandment, as always, receive a great deal of attention.

Most Catholic and Protestant moral theologians now agree that there are actions that must always, or almost always, be avoided. But they are much more restrained and careful about drawing up the list than are *Veritatis Splendor* and the new *Catechism of the Catholic Church.*

Emphasis on absolute prohibitions (all binding under mortal sin) and having a complete list of them becomes crucially important only when the aim is the broadest possible control by the Church and the requirement of confession. In a morality of responsibility, where salvific solidarity sets the tone, the accents are different. Here the supreme focus is on the demands for commitment to peace, justice, and environmental ethics.

Heavy demands, too, are made on the bearers of authority and every individual person. In all this, we assume that it would not be easy to draw up an exhaustive list of every positive and negative duty. To be sure, individual categories must be clearly defined, but without trying to erect a precise boundary between mortal and venial sin. What is crucial, we think, is motivation and concentration on the core areas of responsibility.

But before and beyond focusing on individual acts, we find in a specifically Christian morality the basic intention and basic decision that must become increasingly better and more effectively rooted in continuous repentance. What counts are decisive convictions, basic attitudes (virtues), and character formation to match.

All these are things that external controllers don't care to think about. Still, a continuous self-examination both of individuals and groups or communities is very important. Shared responsibility and solidarity must come first.

From the liturgy and Holy Scripture we are led to ascribe a key role to the historically powerful (eschatological) virtues.

Gratitude is the channel that allows us to participate in all the good of the past. The virtues of *watchfulness*, *preparedness*, and the *gift of discernment* are directed to the present moment of decision. *Hope* and courage to take *responsibility* make the here and now fruitfully receptive for the future.

12
—

Do We Need a Complete List
of Binding Dogmas and Moral
Commandments?

Roman-style moral theology has no parallel either in the
first millennium of the Catholic Church nor in any other
part of the Christian world. It tried to make hairsplitting
distinctions between serious (that is, mortal) and merely venial
sin.

Now we can only shake our heads at all the things that used to
fit under the category of mortal sin. Let me cite just one example
from not very long ago: An *instructio* from the Congregation for
Divine Worship and the Discipline of the Sacraments says concerning Mass without acolytes that if no man can be found, a
woman may say the responses, but only from an appropriate distance: "All authors unanimously teach that women, including nuns,
are forbidden under pain of mortal sin to serve at the *altar*" (AAS
41 [1949] 507–08).

Back when I first read this instruction together with my students, I took the trouble of consulting all the relevant books on
moral theology in our library. We found only two moralists who
taught that women venturing past the communion rail to the altar
were committing mortal sin. But those two were bad enough.

Pope John Paul II and his closest advisers are deeply concerned with teaching believers everything that must be believed and *completely* covering all moral commandments. To their mind, there should be no degrees or nuances in the generic act, although, of course, there may be degrees in the specific performance. The new *Catechism of the Catholic Church* (1994) and the encyclical *Veritatis Splendor* are the two leading papal documents that aim to provide an exhaustive rundown of all religious doctrines and moral norms.

Everywhere in the Christian world people are asking whether this quest for completeness is appropriate or even right. There can be no doubt that we as Christians want to take faith to its height and depth, length and breadth, into our hearts and minds. And we also want to leave no doubt about our desire to carry out the will of God to the best of our ability without cutting corners. Still, it is something else again to make up an encyclopedic list of everything that Catholics have to believe, do, and avoid.

Our question here, however, is quite different and allows a certain variety of positions. In post-Tridentine dogmatic and moral theology the catalogs of what one had to profess in faith or avoid as sin, especially as mortal sin, varied in length. But almost all of them had one thing in common. Dogmatic theologians distinguished carefully, though often controversially of course, an article of faith (*de fide*) or *defined* article of faith *(de fide definita)*, what was considered theologically certain, which doctrines were common and prevalent doctrine, and which were prevalent but not unanimous. The moralists had their precise gradations between undisputed, universal teaching, more or less common doctrine, and more or less probable opinions. The range of controversial opinions—except for the so-called "tutiorists"—was very broad.

Things are altogether different in the two major papal documents we have just been discussing. Here we find the flatfooted assertion, "This is the case," and in the domain of faith and morals we find a host of absolute theses that have won such a resounding affirmation nowhere else in the Christian world— neither from Catholic theologians nor a majority of zealous Catholics.

Anyone thoroughly familiar with the history of dogma and moral theology knows that many ideas once considered definitively settled have later been revised or have just slipped into oblivion. In the realm of morality, historically attested changes are far numerous than in dogmatics.

Much that is flatly rejected today was silently tolerated or even firmly asserted in an earlier day. Rome still allowed the buying and keeping of slaves so as to have them and their children baptized—at a time when the greatest part of the civilized world had already branded slavery as supremely evil.

Simply knowing about this past history of moral certainties should make us more cautious. There is a very rich core of truths of faith and statements about morality on which we in the Catholic Church and even our sister Churches are agreed or could agree. What remains is, naturally, of some importance, but we could and should persevere in fruitful, peaceful dialogue and thus form a community of learning.

More essential points remain to be considered. In the domain of faith, the highest ground is adoring reverence for the absolute *mystery* of the triune God. A reverentially marveling attitude, extremely restrained in words and concepts, has had great and holy representation in the Church. It offends more against the reverence due to faith when we add an iota too much than when we leave a question open. Our words and our whole conceptual world are limited and historically conditioned in many ways, above all when it comes to speaking about God and Christ.

There are still other points of view, which have already been touched on in this book: ecumenism, which has become necessary precisely because parts of the Christian world have made all too many narrow-minded affirmations. This they did from a failure to distinguish between what is essential and what is more or less secondary, between the truth itself and its cultural modes of expression.

The completeness that the new *Catechism of the Catholic Church* (1994) and *Veritatis Splendor* strive for has not (or has not sufficiently) taken into account and shed light on the concerns of ecumenism. Similarly, *inculturation* calls for a heightened reserve in declaring each and every thing obligatory once and for all. How often over the course of Church history—and that includes the history of the missions—have barriers been thrown up because we could not distinguish between the length, height, breadth, and depth of the mystery of faith and human, culturally conditioned concepts and systems.

On the question of how divine foreknowledge and the primacy of grace could be compatible with free human will, such groups as the Molinists and Banesians engaged in fierce verbal swordplay. On the advice of Robert Bellarmine, who himself had escaped condemnation and disciplining by the Inquisition only thanks to papal favor, Clement VIII (1591–1605) refused to make any doctrinal decision. But he bluntly ordered both sides to stop anathematizing each other and to conduct their discussions in a more civilized tone. Nowadays scarcely anyone engages in disputes over this point. Everyone realizes that the ever greater mystery of God forbids us from categorically laying down the law on such matters.

One new feature of the Vatican's current restoration phase is the introduction of truths of faith that are admittedly not revealed but *definitively decided* by the pope. These truths allow neither doubt nor dispute. The Vatican has also introduced what are surely *not* infallible truths in faith and morals that the pope has decided, without giving them the stamp of definitiveness. But no public dissent may be voiced about them.

Yet have not many doctrines once seen and stressed as definitive been modified over the course of the centuries? Haven't many theologians, out of pure fear and under heavy pressure, recanted to the Inquisition, although in their hearts they thought differently? It is something to think about: with all this pressure to retract, how could such a retraction be sincere? What about the conscience of the badgered theologian?

Those who know Church history will find a powerful lesson here: popes can, as in the case of Clement VIII, defuse violent conflicts, but at other times the popes have picked sides and contributed, even if involuntarily, to polarization and splits. I believe that with a better understanding of the Petrine pastoral office, the focus has to be placed more on reconciliation and overcoming divisions.

Only a blind man could fail to see the dangers of polarization facing Catholic moral theology. The system of suspicion, pressure, and polarization was once applied to dogmatic theology (the Modernism controversy), then these tactics were applied to exegesis. Both these areas later witnessed an astonishing and fruitful relaxation of tension. Now moral theology has somehow become the field where everything is at stake: the self-concept of the Church, the office of the pope, ecumenism, and inculturation. In a wider sense, the future itself is at stake. Today's moral theology faces the question, are we to remain the "salt of the earth"?

13

Christian Morality in a Critical Age

Moral theology and the magisterium insofar as it deals with morality have to be aware of their audience and of the mind-set of that audience as it is involved in living the actualities of life.

We live in a critical age, critical above all vis-à-vis religion and its institutions. In addition, there is another important factor. In an age of mass media and sophisticated manipulation of public opinion, Christians must not just have the virtue of discernment; the virtue of criticism must be integrated into their whole character as well. The sharpest criticism of religion, especially of its moral teachings, comes from the many forms of atheism with their infectious and sometimes pugnacious manner.

Consider, by contrast, the enormous difference between the world of the post-Tridentine Catechism and the situation of the direct and indirect audience of the *Catechism of the Catholic Church* (1994). The *Catechism* of the Council of Trent had an easy time of it in comparison. It was aimed at persons who in the stormy era of the Reformation had remained faithful to the Catholic Church. Often, to be sure, such belonging was thanks to the mere accident of princes' opting for that particular church, in keeping with the principle: *"Cujus regio, ejus et religio."* It sufficed that a few hundred bishops and a not much larger number of well-educated theologians accepted the Council of Trent *Catechism* and committed themselves to disseminating its doctrine. Opposite them stood the majority of a poorly educated clergy and the "lay people," who were looked down on as theological ignoramuses.

Things are quite different in our Church today where the number of trained theologians, men and women, and of lay people with considerable competence in theology, is larger than the sum total of competent theologians from all previous centuries. For this very reason, however, the best thing is that clearly the 1994 *Catechism* can look forward to a critical reception. This means that in a simultaneous common effort many readers will be prepared to respect gratefully all the good in the *Catechism*, while separating out what is less good or even mistaken. But the danger then exists that many Catholics will uncritically endorse the rejection of this *Catechism* by well-known theologians; or, perhaps, after critically reading it themselves, they will, thanks to some of its serious flaws, move still further way from the Church's teaching.

Letter to Those Standing Far Off

Cardinal Giovanni Battista Montini, archbishop of Milan and later Pope Paul VI, once sent a pastoral letter to the masses of people who were more or less alienated from the Church. He called it a "Letter to Those Standing Far Off." The letter's tone, concerns, and goals have lost nothing of their relevance today. In a similar state of mind and with a similar pastoral attitude, Cardinal Basil Hume of London publicly begged the forgiveness of divorced and remarried persons for the Church's wrong-headed attitude toward them.

In many dioceses and countries, those "standing far off" from the Church are much more numerous than those who regularly practice their religion. The reasons for, and degrees of, people's alienation differ very widely. Nevertheless, it is foolish and counterproductive to try to explain this distance simply by invoking the "evil world" or, as has often been the case in recent years, the secularization of the Western world.

That explanation does not mean that personal responsibility or even guilt might not be factors for those who stand far off from the Church. But it would be a sign of self-righteousness if we failed to ask *ourselves* why people are keeping their distance from the Church. This question is one that we theologians and preachers of morality—as well as the higher officials in the Church—must face seriously and humbly.

Catholic moral preaching has been largely deficient in *paraclesis*—that is, amiable encouragement in the power of the Holy Spirit with a view to the salvific order of God's gracious love. In addition, critical Catholics have long been put off by the Church's failure to criticize itself. In not a few cases, Catholics have been repelled by the triumphalism of Church officials.

The authorities of the magisterium, at every level, have to face tough questions: In the name of our mission, in the name of God, haven't we all too often said inconsistent things not just casually, but fiercely? The Vatican II Decree on Ecumenism reminds us of something that has a burning relevance far beyond the topic of ecumenical dialogue. In the beginning, it issues a warning to all of us: that when we seek to search together for the divine mysteries, that we always have to proceed "with love for the truth, with charity, and with humility." Then follows the crucial sentence: "They should remember that in Catholic doctrine there exists an order or 'hierarchy' of truths, since they vary in their foundation of the Christian faith." (n. 11).

Generations of rigoristic moral theologians have sinned against this vision and this directive when, as Karl Rahner said, they laid down a verdict of "mortal sin" on trifles. In the past, and up until our day, the Vatican also has badly erred in this matter. I am deliberately avoiding the expression, "seriously sinned." On this important question, however, there is also a kind of "collective guilt" with regard to "sinful structures." Those who fail to do their part to get rid of such structures share the responsibility for them.

If we and church officials would humbly consider our past, there would no longer be any rush to make solemn pronouncements in God's name about rather minor matters, and certainly not about highly debatable doctrines. If all our thinking and speaking were a loving and concerned "letter to those standing far off," a great deal would be gained. For their part, aren't they a letter from God to us?

Challenged by Atheism

Amid much tension and after long hesitation, the Second Vatican Council turned to the problem of atheism with open eyes and a troubled heart. In its various shapes and guises, atheism presents us with many questions. Sometimes it holds up a mirror before our eyes, when we think and talk about God and denying God as if we ourselves were totally untroubled, as if we knew all about God and his will, down to the fine print. From the abundance of relevant statements in *Gaudium et Spes,* I excerpt only one, which is directly linked to the concern for "proclaiming salvation in a critical time":

> For atheism, taken as a whole, is not present in the mind of man from the start. It springs from various causes, among which must be included a critical reaction against religions and, in some places, against the Christian religion in particular. Believers can thus have

more than a little to do with the rise of atheism. To the extent that they are careless about their instruction in the faith, or present its teaching falsely, or even fail in their religious, moral, or social life, they must be said to conceal rather than to reveal the true nature of God and of religion. (*GS* 19).

The commission assigned to produce *Gaudium et Spes* had gathered together on its editorial board over sixty bishops, almost as many theologians, and many alert lay people. This group had a chorus of voices maintaining that the responsibility for fostering atheism didn't lie predominantly or even exclusively with the "believers," but that bad behavior and wrong decisions by Church officials and unhealthy Church structures also had to be examined. But the time was not ripe at that point. There was fear that the already significant resistance to the text of *Gaudium et Spes* would have swollen mightily if the hierarchy had been directly charged with a share in the guilt.

The 1994 *Catechism of the Catholic Church*, which devotes less than a full page to the problem of atheism, quotes the part of the text of *Gaudium et Spes* beginning with the word "believers" (§2125). In this context, too, the guilt seems to lie entirely with ordinary believers.

However, since the Council, a great deal has been thought, spoken, and written on the question of "sinful structures" and sinful misuse of authority. The new *Catechism* would have won much wider agreement if the voice of a self-critical Church authority had been heard in it. There has to be clear witness to the fact of past and present neglect of religious teaching and/or misrepresentation of doctrine by moral theologians and the highest-ranking spokespersons for the magisterium. This is in part simply a tribute to human limitations. Still, when it comes to such contro-

versial issues as placing rightful responsibility for the rise of atheism, the question of a guilty lagging behind cannot and should
not be ignored. I believe that for all those who have suffered from
Roman-style moral theology and warped statements and emphases by representatives of the magisterium, this will become a challenge in the sense of a turning point for growth rather than an
accusation.

Rewards and Punishment in Morality and Education

The mere reduction of the Church's moral teaching to a system
of rewards and punishments has gone a long way to make people
doubt God and drive them into atheism. If, by contrast, we lived
essentially in the consciousness of praise and generosity, in response to the free gift of our chosenness, we could create an invit-
ing, friendly community of believers.

Have we really, however, already overcome a morality based
on rewards and punishments? I doubt that very much. Yet we *are*
on the way to doing so, even in the face of sure and stiff resistance. One large bloc of opposition is the current wave of restoration theology running through our Church.

Back in the nineteenth century, Antonio Rosmini (1797–1855)
made some penetrating remarks about the reward-and-punishment
system in the Church. Above all, Rosmini thought that the yes-men,
the inevitable product of such a system, were wounds in the body of
the holy Church. The problem of the yeasayers was, and always
has been, closely bound up with the striving to impose total conformity far beyond the boundaries of revealed dogmatic and ethical truths. The Inquisition was an especially dubious embodiment
of manipulation through threats and punishments. But it func-
tioned in its harsh way only to the extent that strategies of reward
and promotion produced a large enough supply of yeasayers.

When Rosmini wrote his book on the *Five Wounds of the Church* (1848), the restoration launched by the "Holy Alliance" between the papacy, the czar of Russia, the emperor of Austria, and the king of Prussia, was at its height. The Papal States at that time were a parade ground for manipulation through promises, promotions, and threats of punishment.

Today we have to confront the attempt by another restoration to achieve absolute conformity with all papal teachings (including some that are surely not infallible) through sanctions against nonconformists. This quest for conformity is being carried out in conjunction with a previously unheard-of exercise of power by means of the appointment of bishops and the strictest oversight in filling theological chairs and other Church offices. These events are the key to the current phase of restoration, and no doubt also are its most distinct feature.

Beyond the circle of those who are somehow vulnerable to manipulation and who actually buy into a reward-and-punishment morality, who are left to really serve the Church—its mission, its transparency, its credibility, and its attractiveness? Helpful answers can be given only by those who have discarded this premoral level of "what's in it for me," and have strictly tested themselves to see whether or not they are serving God and the Church selflessly, whether or not this service "gets them something."

For me and for all of us, a ringing appeal is given to live as eucharistic Christians in praise and thanks. And certainly the moral theologians who are oriented to renewal through the overcoming a morality of rewards and punishments still have work to perform—for many people haven't yet gotten a very clear picture of this whole problem.

Citizens of Two Worlds

The Church must take to heart the fact that Christians in the secular world, in politics, culture, and society are supposed to prove themselves responsible adults. The Church wants Christians to refuse to let themselves be manipulated in any area, whether politics or the media, and so on. But it is unthinkable that Christians who are conformists in the Church could at the same time be pioneers of internal and external freedom in the world.

We can and must learn from the past. Lutheran theology before Hitler's day insisted that Christians had to obey secular authority in all things. Originally, these authorities were local princes who had sided with Luther's Reformation. In Prussia, Calvinist rulers found they had subjects who were obedient in good Lutheran fashion. This resulted in a combination of dutiful subjects and rulers with a strong hand. And so the "programmed" pious turned out to be all too pliant followers of Hitler.

Catholic moral doctrine has always taught that one must, when necessary, disobey and even resist the state. But in the final analysis Catholics, like Lutherans, were obedient and susceptible to Hitler. Why? Because in the inner space of the Catholic Church during that era no room existed at all for adult judgment or the courage to contradict.

The bottom line is that the Church needs grown-up Christians, the vanguards of true freedom and responsibility, pioneers in the field of social justice and the politics of peace. It abhors dictatorships. Logically, then, within the Church and, above all, in the varied field of morality, a spirit of mature independence ought to flourish. It should blossom in such a way that Catholic Christians would never play exploitative games with others or let themselves be exploited by them. This is the only way we can be a healing and liberating presence in a critical world.

In all things, in its legislation, its structures, in its internal relations, the Church must be transparent and immune to manipulation. This is especially true insofar as we want to live and be effective under the critical gaze of our contemporary world, particularly young people.

The Courageous Right to Have Sincere Doubts

In the following discussion, we need to keep separate two related questions: first, what is the meaning of doubt as we continue our quest for deeper illumination of the truth? How should this quest be accomplished in a manner that is faithful to the ideals of truth itself? Second, and this is a dramatic question, above all, for theologians, priests, and bishops: may we and should we at times express publicly our doubts and misgivings?

There are lazy doubts, stupid doubts, blasé and frivolous doubts; but that list by no means exhausts the negative arsenal of types of doubt. But there exists also—and there has to be—serious and sincere doubt as an expression of a reverent search for fuller truth.

Good parents and educators always take children's questions seriously, even and especially when they raise doubts. They answer on the child's level and in a way that reflects the seriousness and importance of the question and the doubt. Those who think that in faith and morals every doubt must be banned and tabooed fail to see the great danger of repressed doubts: in the depths of the spiritual life, doubt can cause terrible trouble. In all important areas of life sincere doubts have to be endured and dealt with. That doesn't mean that we should begin by doubting everything. But healthy doubt has its place as an expression of love for the truth and in the striving for fuller knowledge.

Passing on the truth without domineering and all the while resisting every kind of manipulation demands, for one thing, vigilant care to assert nothing *more* than one sincerely thinks one knows. For another thing, such faith does not want to impose the truth, but to lead people to it. Thus doubt must be given breathing space and awarded all of its rights. We have to allow one another, through our entire conduct, room for reciprocal doubting.

Positive doubt can be a first meaningful step toward the affirmation and acquisition of truth. That holds for all historical epochs, but it has special importance and impact in a culture that is both critical and endangered by manipulation. Genuine pedagogy incorporates a wise and timely doubt into the crucial virtue of the discernment of spirits, the virtue of "criticism."

Not every doubt, of course, has to be aired in front of others. One can express serious doubts only to people who won't react allergically to them and who can positively accompany and help positive doubters on the way to more light.

Upright Christians have nothing to be ashamed of when they are sometimes tempted by doubts. But that doesn't mean that we shouldn't pray not to be led into temptation and not to lightly seek or provoke temptation. We should also seek to strengthen one another.

Often enough in my life, especially in recent years, people have asked me whether I was ever troubled by doubts about faith. I think I can sincerely say that to this moment my faith in God, the Almighty Father, and in Christ, the Redeemer, and in the Holy Spirit, the Comforter and Paraclete, has never seriously wavered. This faithfulness certainly has nothing to do with my own merits; it is grace. On the other hand, I have to admit to having had a good many doubts about whether everything that popes, bishops, and theologians teach really belonged to the body of the faith and was suitable to it.

It is part of our task and our service to the Church as moral theologians to take the variety of moral norms that have been or are taught and submit them to scholarly (not necessarily existential) doubt. We must ask whether they were once appropriate and whether they still are appropriate today. This is not challenging for the sake of challenging but a reverential testing in absolute love for truth and goodness.

Yet this task also calls for a certain readiness, after all the probing and testing, to question a specific teaching of the Church. Can I admit this doubt not only in my own thinking and in relation to my own life, but to others' as well? May I or should I voice my doubt publicly? This is a special question that can be answered only in full, shared responsibility for others and the community.

Neither before nor after the Second Vatican Council did I write and publish everything that was on my mind. But I took a great deal of pains not to write anything I believed to be false. I presented nothing as certain that after mature examination seemed doubtful. People who question me about ethical issues, particularly with regard to the Church's teaching, have a right to an honest answer. One serves neither the truth nor the Church through so-called "pious lies."

Our faith and salvific solidarity deserve the highest possible degree of openness. Our fellow Christians have a right to know what the Church's moral theologians think about the existential questions that concern them. They have a right to ask us whether we ourselves are really convinced by the Church's arguments on a particular issue. If we dodge these existential questions without good reason, we are cowards. If we give insincere answers, to avoid disturbing our sleep or our career, we are swindlers, worse than merchants who pass on counterfeit money.

But Are There No Controls?

Of course there are. Just as every complicated piece of machinery needs a safety valve, when it comes to the truths of faith, even though in a totally different way, we need precautions to protect ourselves and others from dangerous errors and deceptions.

In the first place, I would say that silence and questioning in prayer before God are an indispensable safety valve. We need a living awareness of responsibility before the face of God. The second safety valve is sincere dialogue, conversation with wise and pious fellow Christians and colleagues. One of the surest and most indispensable safety valves is civilized discussion with other theologians, in person or in professional journals. We should not just be accessible to serious criticism, but grateful for it.

This unceasing dialogue takes place under the eyes of the magisterium. If it is carried out in a healthy Church atmosphere, it will have a purifying, healing, enlightening, and liberating character. By contrast, if I know that a certain theologian is viewed as dangerous by his bishop or by Rome and that he or she has been threatened with sanctions, then in most cases I will have to avoid doing anything that might add fuel to the fire. Even so, too many and too harsh controls promulgated from above throw the "horizontal" safety valves out of kilter and damage their effectiveness.

In terms of reciprocal correction, once again the principle of subsidiarity applies. Whatever can be solved on the level of theological discussion does not need harsh intervention from on high. Whatever can be cleared up on the regional level of any given culture should not be regulated through interference by the central authorities. This empowerment is especially vital when the central authorities are not familiar with, or are not fully familiar, with the culture and life of the region.

The Liberating "Nevertheless" of Praise

A morality founded on grace and healing, on liberating nonviolence will flourish and prevail within a praising Church. A truly eucharistic Church does not turn back beneath the whip of threatening legalism. It also does not flag in times of crisis, but will be ever more keenly aware that a crisis can and must be turned into a phase of growth.

If we sing together with all generations and with the heavenly powers, "You alone are holy. You alone are the Most High, Jesus Christ," then a ridiculous and pretentious impressiveness and the temptation to maximize our own power can no more tempt us than a crude reward-and-punishment morality.

Only insofar as we let ourselves be caught up, with all our mind, heart, and energy, in the praise of the redeemed, do we stand on the solid ground of morality, of grace, and of liberating love. There is healing frankness only in the powerful flow of praise. Even well-meant attempts at reform are doomed to fail unless they are undergirded and enveloped by the spirit of praiseful gratitude. Criticism of the Church without ongoing praise for God's wondrous deeds and promises turns sour and makes people despondent.

Still, room exists in this praising for sighing and complaining. On this point the Psalms—the Book of Praise, as Martin Buber calls it—give us some good insights. A praising community never remains stuck in moaning or criticizing. It is always launching out on a new departure toward attitudes and action that redound to the honor of God and the salvation of human beings.

Part II

—

The Turnaround
Looms on the Horizon

History was always my favorite subject. To me the most interesting part of moral theology was its stories; dogmatic theology likewise took on a special interest because of the history of dogma. How could I understand the Church without looking into its history? The study of history, as I see it, is not primarily retrospective, but the most intensive view of *the here and now*, whose contours become visible against the background of the past.

Anyone fascinated by the variety and dynamism of the whole history of the human race will be forever teased by the question: where will we humans go from here? I have even noticed this already in my own individual life: medical crises in my personal history have more than once—in retrospect—proved to be turning points; sickness was a way to experience new health and power. This fact has appeared to me, sometimes even in dreams, as a source of astonishingly hopeful joy.

My readers might be worrying now that, as I begin the second part of this book trying to understand and interpret further aspects of the present-day Church, I will be serving up dreams, though perhaps of the waking kind. Well, why not? For me dreams are not something minor or meaningless. Often—again in my personal experience—while enjoying a high degree of good health, I have had wonderful, beautiful dreams. In them, everything comes together as I had hoped for. When my health is shaken, my dreams are usually a muddle. But that muddle doesn't make me pessimistic in the least because, after all, I know how to take dreams simply as dreams.

Sometimes when I am wide awake I also indulge in dreams about the Church, which can be as passionate as my love for the Church. But I critically scrutinize these daydreams by myself and with others. Are they based on hard reality? Is their point of departure a careful analysis of the most recent present? Can these imaginings be verified to some extent by comparison with models from past history?

Next comes what is most important for me—the question to my conscience: will I, along with my friends, do everything to try to realize at least a part of these necessary dreams? Will I examine my thoughts, words, and actions to see if they can be steps to the better future that I long for?

When I was a coworker on the preparatory commissions for the Second Vatican Council, I wouldn't let myself get depressed by negative experiences. When there was absolutely no progress being made, no movement at all, I held on. I had a natural instinct, and a grace too, no doubt: I always saw, first and foremost, the encouraging signs of the time. And even back then there were plenty of them. For all my reservations about Hegel's reading of history, in which thesis and antithesis always lead to a synthesis, I see a great deal of meaning in it. Anyone who experiences a historical epoch, where the dynamic of thesis and antithesis clearly manifests itself, can dare to hope, after close inspection of the whole picture, for a new synthesis. And that is the case right now.

At the Second Vatican Council, two religious and cultural visions of history crashed into each other. The Council came to a surprisingly rich synthesis, even though, in some ways, still a fragile one. Further construction will continue upon this foundation.

In the epoch of restoration that is the pontificate of John Paul II, an antithesis—though not a complete one—has been taking shape. It is not strong enough simply to steamroll the synthesis achieved by the Council. In my view, however, it has made such deep inroads into the historical image of the Church that, having now exhausted itself as an antithesis, it is stretching out toward a more vigorous synthesis of its own. In my interpretation, in the last years of the pontificate of Karol Wojtyla an old model has largely run itself into the ground, thus paving the way for a turnaround that is in the offing. What this will look like depends upon everyone involved in the process, including moral theologians. A new course is taking shape, while old and new energies are becoming more clearly perceptible.

One feature of the new course that can scarcely be overestimated is the new possibilities of shaping public opinion. The Church is facing a dynamic challenge to achieve a heightened, in some ways altogether new, transparency. Without that candor, healthy renewal is quite unthinkable. I see the challenge, above all, in the problem of influencing public opinion in and through the Church.

The protagonists of partial restoration have been and are two highly gifted men, Karol Wojtyla and Joseph Ratzinger. Both have made masterful use of the modern media. In many ways they are men of unusual energy and talent. Both experienced the Council as participants and effectively promoted certain measures there. Behind them stood (and stand) many pious believing Catholics, people for whom obedience and tightly structured order are the foundational values of the Church. Not a few such men and women were moved to accept the Council in principle, though only in a modified version, thanks to the restrictive interpretation of it by these two leading figures.

I suspect that many supporters of Pope Wojtyla's line will be followers of the next pope, even if that man winds up leading the Church out of certain narrow positions. They will no doubt gradually learn that their obedience must increasingly reflect the more comprehensive paradigm of responsibility—personal and shared.

I also fear, however, that the coming phase of Church history will have to deal with some "hazardous wastes" from past attempts to interpret the Council in a restrictive, restorational mode. These pollutants with which we have to cope are not just in people's heads, but in a whole series of troublesome structures. For the past twenty years, the structures of power and control in the Church have been so overemphasized and underlined that they can now be quite readily identified by many of our contemporaries. Thus they can now be unmasked and recognized as obsolete.

14

The Power of Public Opinion

One of the greatest achievements of the modern democracies is freedom of expression. The nineteenth-century popes were still outspoken opponents of freedom of speech. Despite this prohibition, the First Vatican Council became the occasion of vehement public dispute.

A turnaround in the Church's official position began with Leo XIII. Not until the pontificate of Pius XII, however, did a pope spoke out frankly and emphatically in favor of the free play of public opinion inside the Catholic Church. In an important address on February 20, 1950, this pope stressed that, like secular society, the Church also needed a healthy public exchange of opinion: "Something would be missing in its inner life, if public opinion were missing—a situation where the fault would reflect on the shepherds as well as the faithful."

Freedom of speech in society and the Church is emphasized still more clearly in the Decree on the Means of Social Communication. Vatican II as a whole might be said to be a constructive explosion of public opinion. This exchange of opinion was true not just inside the Council hall and the committee rooms, but all over the world, in all circles and almost all organs of public opinion.

This qualitative advance was apparent to anyone who could compare the stifling air in most of the Curia-dominated preparatory commissions with the experience of the Council. It was something like a feast of sincerity in thought and speech. Hand in hand with this went a new passion in the quest for truth and the apposite expression of it.

The power of free speech was later given exemplary illustration after the encyclical *Humanae Vitae* on birth control. Pope Paul VI and the Roman Curia were quite surprised by the nature of the response. One indication of the greatness of Paul VI is that he neither undertook nor authorized repressive measures. Not until the end of his pontificate did the Congregation of the Faith again go into high gear in an attempt (which basically failed) to suppress deviant minorities.

The pontificate of John Paul II, by contrast, has been marked by a whole series of measures aimed at cutting off all reactions, except positive ones, to papal pronouncements. Theologians, especially moralists, have again and again been admonished to make the pope's statements the strict guideline for all their efforts. The chief, if not the only, concern here is sexual ethics, on which the pope has had a great deal to say.

In this context, of course, we have Pope John Paul's remarks on the supposed incapacity of women for the priesthood. To impose a consensus on this matter, the strongest methods were used. The weightiest of these is the loyalty oath to the papal magisterium, which goes far beyond the area of infallible teachings on faith and morals.

If priests and theologians take this oath, as demanded, then if they ever dissent they can also be charged with violating their oath. This turn of events is something absolutely new. Up until now, the German Bishops' Conference has not commented on the issue; evidently they are convinced that calling for such an oath is unreasonable. Seminarians from a diocese where the bishop insisted on their taking it came to me for advice: could they swear the oath despite inner reservations in order to make sure that they were admitted to the priesthood?

The dilemma is distressing. I thought of my own scruples when I had to take the old oath against Modernism. The representatives of the Curia on the preparatory Congregation of the Faith wanted all the conciliar fathers to renew the anti-Modernist oath at the beginning of the Council. It was a liberating moment when John XXIII decided that no oath would be required. Many people heaved a sigh of relief shortly afterward when the oath was abolished altogether.

But the loyalty oath to the papal magisterium is not the only repressive measure. In fact, a grandiose total strategy has been mobilized, with screening of all theologians on these controverted doctrines. I know a whole group of theologians from all over the world who have had their permission to teach denied or rescinded because of remarks they have made on this topic.

The core of the papal strategy "for safeguarding unity," however, lies in the careful selection of candidates for bishop on the basis of their loyalty to the pope. Above and beyond that, whenever necessary, it has been made clear to all bishops that they have to behave and speak in conformity with Rome. Thus, for example, the former bishop of Rottenburg, Georg Moser, told me that the pope harangued him about the German bishops having to recant the so-called Königstein declaration on *Humanae Vitae*. Moser explained to me that he flatly rejected this demand, which he saw as outrageous. But the inevitable question arises: in a similar or the same situation, how many bishops would be so bold and speak so freely?

For me and for many other people these days, the "Gaillot case" is one of the clearest signs of the changeover that is in the air. The pope and his closest collaborators have plainly announced that they want to impose conformity even on matters unrelated to any clear-cut truth of faith. Fearless expression of one's own convictions and innovative pastoral practice have been branded as "dissent." For a long time now, this word, thanks to loyalty oaths and punitive sanctions, has evoked in many people's minds the impression of a "threatening Church."

Many sources confirm that Gaillot never said or did anything heretical. He and his many friends are distinguished by the pains they take to be perfectly open and aboveboard, by a conscientious avoidance of "diplomatic" language. There was also his cheerful faith and his dedication to evangelical nonviolence. I have never heard Gaillot accused of saying a harsh word, much less an insult, against the pope.

Bishop Gaillot was assigned a defunct diocese in the wilderness as his episcopal see. That action signaled what kind of a blatant changeover was in the offing. However the desert began to bloom and voices were heard on all sides, saying "We belong to Partenia." Of late, Bishop Gaillot has appeared on the Internet, and so Partenia has become a verdant diocese, without checkpoints, without a bureaucracy, but with a very high degree of dialogue.

The turnaround was reflected no less clearly in the conflict involving bishops Lehmann, Saier, and Kasper from the Upper Rhine. These three men got into trouble because of a very moderate, nuanced effort to get something started in the pastoral care of divorced people. They wanted a policy to match the current state of theology and that would meet today's special needs. It was no more than a cautious step toward the *oikonomia* of the Orthodox Churches.

Three times these bishops had to make a pilgrimage to Rome; and it is widely suspected that the pope's reaction would have been much harsher if Cardinal Ratzinger had not served as mediator. But the crucial part of this event, once again, is that the three bishops behaved with absolute dignity, sincerity, honesty, and nonviolence. Hence the turnaround has an authentic evangelical quality about it.

Both episodes met with an unprecedented worldwide response, which greatly increased their impact. Especially important, it seems to me, was the rather gentle echo they had in English Catholicism. The highly respected, modest, distinguished Cardinal Basil Hume made a public apology for the injustice done to divorced people by a crudely undifferentiated pastoral approach.

What Pius XII announced in a general way about the irreplaceable role of public opinion is now unmistakably and powerfully clear—not least of all because of the Vatican's furious efforts to impose a consensus, if need be, by brutal measures.

Catholics no longer simply accepted talk about "unity" (which actually was just aimed at enforcing conformity). On the contrary, the whole problem of all the steps designed to guarantee conformity now met with well-coordinated criticism. The new forces at work could be observed and felt as practically never before. Thanks to the possibility of forthright public exchanges, the "sleeping giant" spoken of by a conciliar observer for the Methodists, had awakened.

After long hesitation, the model of church leadership in place until halfway through the twentieth century decided it wanted critical (to a degree) and discerning Christians in government and society. Within the Church, however, everything continued to be focused on the dutiful, uncritically obedient "subject." All statements by the pope were to receive absolutely uncritical obedience and unwavering agreement.

In the present time, we need to recall how catastrophically all this worked out in the context of Nazism. The now obsolescent model of the laity called for a "split Christian": the lay person was supposed to exercise a virtue in the secular world that was taboo inside the Church—the virtue of criticism. But all our virtues depend upon whether Christians distinguish themselves in the whole of historically appropriate action and thought by conscious responsibility, discernment, and frankness. Within the Church, too, the conviction must spread that the Spirit of God "works in all and through all."

Having noted that, we must not overlook what is probably the most serious phenomenon: the growing religious distress in the face of outrageous demands made in pronouncements that surely do not belong to the core of Christian faith. We must concentrate instead on the sure core.

In the rather inglorious history of the Inquisition and its legal successors, harsh pressure was applied (evidently with a "good conscience") to obtain, not to say extort, recantations and declarations of conformity. The question of whether such statements could be made in good conscience obviously never came up. This model was in operation—that is, it got the job done—until very recently.

In this area, I believe, we have to talk about sinful structures. Those who could change them but who do nothing out of dishonest motives or more or less culpable blindness bring on themselves a burden of sin. Up until Vatican II, this system was so efficient because all those who in their sincerity fell afoul of it were treated in their church environment as "lepers." Some of them spoke with me about it. Quite a few of their fellow victims had broken down under the experience.

The more recent attempts to impose conformism through loyalty oaths and various forms of pressure are likewise doomed to fail. That is because a new solidarity within the Church, above all, within the theological community, is on the rise.

This solidarity by no means adds up to a revolt against the pope's authority. There is, in fact, a high degree of readiness to hear the pope out and to ponder his statements seriously. The spiritual space for this listening to the pope is listening as a community to the *Paraclete*, the Holy Spirit, the Encourager, and grateful appreciation of the Spirit's gift of *parrhesia*, or frankness. Loyalty to him who said "You have one teacher" (Mt 23:8) gives rise to an intensive listening to the entire people of God. That means, above all, listening to the poor and, not least of all, to those who have fallen or who are in danger of falling by the wayside.

The Church of Christ is not characterized by an artificial, cleverly devised unanimity. Instead, voices flow together, for all their variety, in love. There is a common effort to interpret the signs of the times and to penetrate more deeply into the truth of faith. Once all the structures of mistrust fall away, openness grows in mutual correction and in the act listening to one another.

After all the painful experiences we have had, we can firmly say: there is no going back to a double paradigm. We cannot have an ethic of responsibility for the secular world and an uncritical ethic of obedience for the Church. The Church has to acknowledge the dignity of conscientiousness and total sincerity. The painful and tragic experiences in the Third Reich, which went far beyond Germany, should have long ago taught us a lesson for the life of the Church and its task in the world.

The Church's strategy of unification by compelling agreement with its own dicta through loyalty oaths and threatened sanctions has come to grief once and for all. The desires of the laity all over the world have made that only too clear. The "sleeping giant," once known as "stupid lay people," has awakened as the people of God. It shakes and jolts those who are still snoring away. A new, although sometimes painful, order is awakening. We may say with complete confidence: the old model of the Church is on the way out, a new world is clearly taking shape.

The pope, who wished to steer the bark of Peter with a strong hand, suffers from the current situation and vehemently complains about the "counter-magisterium." That is a bitter misunderstanding. There *is* a group of upright bishops, countless theologians, and so-called lay people distinguished by their competence both in theology and the most important social sciences. But they by no means think of themselves as a "counter-magisterium." They know that they have been called into service by the magisterium pure and simple, that is, by the one Teacher and Master, Jesus Christ. They have been animated and encouraged by the one Paraclete, who works through the variety of his gifts and charisms. They listen to the magisterium of the saints and to prophetic voices authenticated by courage and humility. They listen to the poor, the rejected, the cry of the plundered planet earth. And, of course, they listen, though critically, to the voice of the pope.

In many ways, when it comes to the major issues, these theologians and lay people listen to the pope more attentively than to well-behaved yes-men. As an example, I have just now seen a book by Bernard Fraling entitled *Sexual Ethics: An Essay From a Christian Perspective*. There is no trace here of a counter-magisterium, but rather a sensitive listening to many voices, considerations, and experiences with a focus on the "one Master." All these serve the whole people of God and hence they perform the task assigned them by the pope.

The cultivation of absolute sincerity and transparency within the Church is strongly motivated by our concern that the Church has to be found believable by a critical world. That critical world wants to see clearly that all of us as a whole and every single individual as well are passionate seekers for truth and hence credible partners in dialogue. It is a tragic error for anyone to think that the crucial elites in today's world would let themselves be even slightly awed by blanket conformism in the Church.

Open exchange of opinions, readiness for dialogue, and absolute sincerity are also indispensable for the service to ecumenical reconciliation. Suppose that in official ecumenical dialogue only the pope's doctrinal ideas were put forward, even if they differed greatly from the theology of the Church as a whole. In that case, the whole undertaking would be doomed.

The parts of Christendom still separate from us have a right to ask critically whether the Catholic Church is a reliable community of learning on all its levels. Only in this way we can move forward, in the face of the one Master and Teacher, to reconciled unity amid healthy variety. But if the separated brothers and sisters couldn't help noticing that within the Catholic Church systematic pressure was being exerted toward conformity, their discouragement would be only too understandable.

I have the impression that, after all, theologians everywhere have passed with dignity the hard test to which they were recently subjected. Sincerity and willingness to dialogue are winning on a broad front. The horizon has widened. Despite the pressure from Church authorities for a less than perfectly sincere uniformity, in general one hardly senses a mood of "anti-magisterium" or rebellion. The depth, breadth, and width of ecumenical willingness to learn is growing. The voice of Rome is not heard in detached isolation, but against the broad horizon of listening to the word of God and the Lord of history.

If theologians succeed through hard work and constant care for dialogue in making the many new insights and reflections available for everyone, then they will be serving the whole Church, the whole Christian world, indeed all of humanity. Needless to say that also means that they are a part of the pope's service to the quest for truth and unity.

Free speech is a pressing concern for the Church on all levels. We are living in an age of the media, of worldwide communication through many voices, shapes, and channels, in an era that is both critical and exposed to manipulation. What may we and should we expect from the Church on this score?

I'll try to answer this question briefly. The Church as a whole has to be a prophetic voice, a messenger of liberating truth, a place of frank and free exchange of opinion, a teacher of discernment (the virtue of criticism). In all this the most crucial factor is not what sort of messages the Church's leadership sends the world; much more important is whether the Church, on every level, is a model of transparency and unmanipulated dialogue.

The Church must realize dynamically and concretely its ideal character as a model of openness. If that gets stripped away, then all the fine declarations about freedom, all the doctrines about free structures are or would be at best ineffective, and at worst offensively provocative.

This whole complex of issues first thrust itself into public consciousness in the light of demands by the laity, first in Austria and Germany, then in many other countries. This wasn't a plebiscite on the truths of faith, but a powerful public event of free speech about issues affecting the welfare of the entire Church.

A great many bishops have not behaved very heroically on this matter. One often hears the suggestion that these men are "squinting," that is, they look first to the Vatican and listen and dare to think and then say only what would "go down well" there.

I am convinced that the desire of the laity for free and frank exchange of opinion in the Church and the world is a prominent sign of the changeover to a new Church. If the Church's leadership were to close itself to this "sign of the time," it would lose a good deal of authority, credibility, and attractiveness.

I am confident that these events will contribute to the Church's introduction of sympathetic structures for the flow of opinion in the Church. Then the Church can also hope to better fulfill its vocation as a prophetic voice for the world.

15

Structures and Formative Principles of the Church

P ope John XXIII and the Second Vatican Council that he called refused to make any infallible declarations. This free and carefully reflected decision no doubt strengthened their authority and credibility.

Under the pontificate of John Paul II, by contrast, much has been written on all sides about "creeping infallibilism"—in recent years, the word "galloping infallibilism" has been used. The tone and language of not a few statements by the pope in his last encyclicals lie close to the edge of infallible decrees. More and more often one hears that this pope is highly conscious of his infallibility. I shall speak at greater length, in the section on the role of women in the Church, about the failed attempt at "infallibilizing" on the issue of the ordination of women. This statement is relevant here only with regard to healthy power structures in the Church.

The First Vatican Council was, and is to this day, an unfinished council, although Vatican II took up many of its key questions. The whole complex of issues concerning primacy of jurisdiction and papal infallibility is the main stumbling block to ecumenism; but it is just as much a source of problems within the Church. It's encouraging that the current pope admitted this quite clearly in his encyclical *Ut Unum Sint*, while expressing his willingness to enter into dialogue on the matter.

Despite vehement, passionate resistance by the old curial guard, the Second Vatican Council addressed and reflected profoundly on the topic of collegiality, but in its understandable effort to reach quasiunanimity in its resolutions, some dubious compromises had to be swallowed. I was one of the many conciliar theologians firmly convinced that the dynamic unleashed by the Council would ultimately lead to effective decentralization, unequivocal subsidiarity, and powerful collegiality. That outcome actually could have occurred, but things worked out differently from what we had hoped.

Probably never before in the history of the Church had such a centralized apparatus of power developed as it has under the long pontificate of John Paul II. In the long run, however, it seems that the watchword Pope John gave for the future by means of his whole example will finally have a far-reaching effect.

Historically, the gradual increase in the power of the Bishop of Rome has sometimes matched the secularization of the papacy stride for stride. Nowadays Gregory the Great (d 604) might well teach us the path to *evangelical moderation*. Gregory was intent on not diminishing in any way the influence, honor, and authority of the traditional patriarchates. After all, bishops and popes, as the New Testament plainly tells us, are not copies of earthly rulers. They are called to be imitators of the humble Servant of God. They should not try to impose through magnificent display and splendid titles, but should invite others to simplicity even in the exercise of their office.

Pope Paul VI brought the Council to an end with skill and sensitivity. He shared in the afterglow of his simple predecessor, and rightly so. His biggest mistake, no doubt, was letting himself be pressured by his advisors into rejecting the overwhelming majority on the commission studying birth control—a commission that he himself had named.

By tying himself down to the vote of commission's minority, he obliged the entire Church to follow his lead. He could easily have left the question open. No one would have held it against him if he had publicly announced that he agreed with the minority. Pope Paul was surprised and shaken by the powerful wave of protests stirred up by his declaration. But he gave, in my opinion, a fine demonstration of pastoral tolerance, respecting the conscience of believers.

A different reaction emerged from the hard core of his advisers, who had pushed the pope into making that tragic decision. Among those advisers was Karol Wojtyla, part of the minority on the commission. How much pain the Church would have been spared if people in Rome had finally given up the hard line.

The successor of Saint Peter doesn't have to be the best theologian. His supreme task is to give infectious witness to faith in Jesus Christ, the Servant and Son of God and, as pastor, to promote unity amid difference. The unity of the Church has never come to grief from confessing the basic truths. Trouble has arisen from splits over matters that could have been left undecided for a while without doing any harm to the witness to the Gospel.

In this context, a first and great step in a new direction could be a plainer definition both of the primacy of jurisdiction as well as of papal-collegial infallibility. On all levels, particularly on the highest one of the brotherhood of the apostles' successors, dialogue has to be conducted humbly and openly. All major decisions have to be supported by the synod of bishops.

The Roman *apparat* has to be downsized. We could do without cardinals altogether. The pope himself should not appoint the men who will choose his successor. The powers and responsibilities of the conferences of bishops and their regional assemblies have to be enhanced. The election of the pope has to be internationally representative, with women participating, for example, on behalf of international Catholic women's organizations.

Likewise, a new set of rules for choosing bishops must be drawn up in accordance with the model of the Church's first millennium. I see no reason why every choice of a bishop has to be scrutinized and confirmed by Rome. Here, too, we could readily borrow models from the first millennium.

Even under these assumptions, the Bishop of Rome would still have more than enough to do. Only the most important responsibility might be mentioned: to be a worldwide model as the diocesan Bishop of Rome and metropolitan, and eventually in the exercise of a patriarchate limited, perhaps, to Italy. The pope could also serve as an umpire in the whole Catholic world, whenever there was a need for a supreme arbitrator.

The Bishop of Rome would be a central point in ecumenical efforts for unity. Through regular synods, whose president would naturally be the Bishop of Rome, whatever urgent issues faced the entire Church would be addressed and, if necessary, decided.

Out of the ashes of the old Congregation for the Doctrine of the Faith a wholly new one might arise, in close cooperation with the corresponding commissions of the conferences of bishops and regional assemblies. Perhaps it would also become an organ at the disposal of the bishops synod, which could be the actual advisory body for the pope.

In such a system, would the pope also have to be the highest theological master, the embodiment of the "magisterium" in the strict sense? Not necessarily. In any case, it would be tremendous if the pope were the incarnation of the Church as *teacher*, always with an eye to Christ: "You have one Master, the Christ."

In view of the fact that a great many people today are privileged to reach an advanced age, it ought to be quite obvious that the Bishop of Rome should be elected only for a limited term. On the issue of retirement age, at least, he would have to be treated just like the other bishops of the world. The Diocese of Rome and the worldwide Church have the right to a pope who can fulfill his responsibilities in perfect health.

I can't imagine that an ecumenically accepted (or acceptable) Bishop of Rome would waste his precious time on anything as idle as the appointment of honorary papal prelates; the byword for the Bishop of Rome in the future will be evangelical simplicity.

16

The Future of the Church
and the Issues of Women

Among the most burdensome legacies of the papacy, along with its broad assimilation to monarchical and absolutistic secular modes of rule, is its patriarchal bias toward the position and dignity of women. Among the undeniable achievements of modernity, by contrast, is the increasing democratization almost everywhere on earth and, along with it, the recognition of the complete equality of women.

On both points, the Catholic Church can and must catch up, remembering the apostolic age and looking constantly to Jesus. The Church as a whole and the Church of Rome in particular must admit, in shame and repentance, that when it comes to the role and dignity of women it has practically always adhered to the sexism of the time. I believe that the spirit of the Gospel in recent days has done its share to enhance the social position of women, but the leadership of the Church hardly deserves much credit for that.

One example will suffice: for a quarter century I was a spiritual adviser of a secular institute of women, some of whom had leadership roles in their professions. All the elder members with university degrees had managed to get these degrees only by resisting the orders of their bishops. They had studied at universities as profoundly religious young women, but in a meaningful act of disobedience to their bishops. It is a miracle that these women were nevertheless animated by such great love for the Church as it actually was. In part, I ascribe this to Cardinal Michael von Faulhaber, who as a young bishop advised them and learned from them what the position and responsibility of Catholic women in the world could be.

In a few German dioceses today, there are some senior women officials on key committees but the Vatican doesn't have a single woman in a responsible post. When it came to admitting women to university careers, the Vatican served only as a brake on progress. One may well say that on women's issues the Roman Church is miles behind secular society.

Nevertheless, in the global Church a great awakening can be seen on the horizon. There are now thousands of highly qualified women theologians, and their number is rapidly growing. What would the Church be without its countless women religion teachers and catechists? To a large extent women are already on the pastoral front lines, that is, in the Andes, where hundreds of parishes and other pastoral centers are single-handedly run by generous women pastors. This is an office for which they have been named, solemnly blessed, and assigned by their bishop.

The superstition, still virulent in my youth, that women are less gifted than men is fortunately extinct almost everywhere now. The world has taken giant steps toward change on that score, but sadly it must be stressed that the Church's authorities remain far behind.

The issue of ordaining women is surely not the whole point in this life-and-death question for the Church. In my opinion, the highest church authority ought to have been exercised patiently; and a wait-and-see attitude should have been adopted. But the fact that churchmen still deny women so categorically the capacity to be ordained is proof enough that on the issue of women the Church has by no means come to grips with its past. This is something it must do in all humility.

Against this background, the "definitive" decision by John Paul II came as a bolt from the blue, even as it was widely acknowledged that the attempt by the Congregation for the Defense of the Faith to categorically exclude any possibility of ordaining women (see *Inter Insigniores* [1977]) had finished itself off by its own lame argumentation. Still more surprising was the declaration by the highest authorities of the Congregation for the Defense of the Faith that the pope's "definitive" *No* was an "infallible" decision. This question shows quite clearly how the problem of simultaneous unsimultaneity is a most serious phenomena in the Church today.

In "splendid isolation," the pope pronounces "infallibly." He and his advisers were evidently unaware of the consequences. The decision was not just untimely, but unnecessary and unhelpful. No one would have resented it if the pope—especially in view of the tensions within the Anglican Church—had observed that the Catholic Church need to take its time until, through patient dialogue, a definite consensus could be reached one way or another.

One sometimes hears people say that the pope's decision on the ordination of women might actually promote reconciliation with the Orthodox Churches. I don't think so. The fact that a pope acting entirely on his own proclaims a new dogma without making sure of his case within his own Church is a much graver occurrence than the problem of ordaining women per se.

I consider Rome's "infallible" decision not only inopportune, but out of touch with the times. The pope's decision actually comes "too late." The emotional frontier on this issue has already been crossed, but in such a way that now even raising the question theo-retically seems a step backward.

There was a time when nuns never left the cloister and couldn't even work as nurses, when there were still no women theologians. If the pope had delivered his categorical *No* back then, it might not have created much of a fuss.

But now the situation is long overdue for rethinking. The Prot-estant and Anglican Churches have risked the experiment of or-daining woman and have gotten good results. They have thought through and discussed the theological question from every angle. Their initiative and their theology have also found an echo in the Catholic Church. The great majority of theologians, particularly the exegetes, have resolutely concluded that Holy Scripture and sound theology fail to support misgivings about the ordination of women. Polls in different countries have revealed that only a mi-nority now considers ordaining women impossible. A decisive factor in this change of mood is the concrete experience of women as very good pastoral caregivers.

Against this background one wonders: what are we actually waiting for? In official, solemn ceremonies the Church has given women the mission and the blessing for crucial pastoral assign-ments, including the task of running whole parishes. Women bap-tize, preach, lead penitential services, attend to the spiritual needs of the sick and dying, and so on. Scholarly studies have shown that back in the Middle Ages the Church acknowledged the au-thority of abbesses to hear confessions and give absolution in their communities. In fact, women are often the more gifted reconcilers.

The crucial point really remains whether women can be autho-rized to say the words of consecration in the Eucharist and call down the Holy Spirit upon the offerings. But, after all, the priest isn't the one who "transubstatiates." He simply invokes the Holy Spirit, who alone can transform the eucharistic offerings. As far as calling down the Spirit goes, how are women inferior to men? If the (male) priest says: "This is my body," that has nothing to do with his masculinity. He isn't speaking in his own name. A woman can cultivate eucharistic gratitude and eucharistic memory just as well as a man.

I suspect that the rejection of ordaining women to celebrate the Eucharist is, after all, a relic of magical thinking. I wouldn't necessarily argue that male opponents of the ordination of women are still bedeviled by the old-time, deeply rooted fear of women's cultic "impurity." However, in critically dealing with our tradition, that point has to be mentioned. This, though, is my main concern: opponents of the ordination of women have yet to come to terms with the burdens of the past—and in the meantime they still aren't ready to do so.

The pope's sudden attempt to "infallibilize" greatly surprised the public. Conversely, his surprise at that reaction was probably just as great. The question now is, "Have we really gotten a new dogma through the pope's declaration?" No one would claim that it is an old dogma, because the Church has never wanted to decide this question dogmatically. Vague opinions, even when they happen to be circulating in many people's heads, do not add up to a dogma.

Some answer the question this way: "What we have here is a botched dogma, so we know that the pope isn't infallible; or, rather, now we finally know that the dogma of infallibility is false." For good reasons I do *not* go along with this argument. I would even maintain that in the case of papal infallibility there are plenty of safety valves. Perhaps in the future we shall have to find still plainer forms of protection against a dubious infallibilism.

With countless men and women who have already expressed their opinion, I maintain that the pope's ideas and personal convictions are taken seriously. But his attempt at infallibilizing his viewpoint has plainly backfired, because he did not stick with the findings and conditions of the magisterium. It was not the Second Vatican Council, but the First, that created safety measures clearly drawing the limits within which infallible papal statements are legally possible.

The most important text in this regard is the constitution *Pastor Aeternus (Eternal Shepherd)* of the First Vatican Council. It reads: "The popes of Rome, in accord with the time and circumstances, have defined what must be firmly believed in agreement with Holy Scripture and apostolic traditions. But they have done so only after determining this through ecumenical councils or investigating the conviction of the Church dispersed all over the earth, for example through particular synods and other means made possible by divine Providence."

The pope did none of that. Otherwise he could have easily discovered that the great majority of exegetes have already said that Scripture offers no proof that it is impossible to ordain women. He really should have known that in many countries a considerable majority of believers consider ordaining women possible or even insist upon it. The believers of every rank who think ordaining women theologically impossible must be in the minority. Of course, this doesn't mean that everyone who sees it as theologically possible positively wants it.

Future historians will argue whether the pope and/or his advisers were aware of this fact. The respected church historian Carlo Zizzola notes in *Rocca*, a Catholic magazine published in Assisi, that the declaration on ordaining women was a "coup" (*colpo di mano*) by a certain group of men in the Vatican. We are looking at a mystery.

Another train of thought moves from similar theological reflections to the same conclusion. In this area, one can rely on thorough studies by Yves Congar, the great theologian whom Pope John Paul II himself made a cardinal. This is the carefully articulated theory of "reception." According to Congar and the many theologians who cite him, a papal teaching can count as definitive and infallible only insofar as it finds a "reception," that is, free assent, in the entire Church. If it finds no such assent, then the pope has most likely not "received" the sense of the faithful on the question. In this case that lack of reception is quite obvious.

Both lines of thought complete and confirm one another on the ordination of women. They back the conviction that despite the pope's undeniable intention of proclaiming an infallible doctrine, no such thing took place. Here is a situation that will doubtless earn a place in the history of the papacy. And it is unlikely that anything similar will "happen" to one of John Paul II's successors.

The failed campaign for the idea that Scripture holds women incapable of the priesthood has involuntarily led to more passionate efforts to clarify the issue everywhere in the Church. I have no doubt that this will work out in favor of ordaining women.

The award-winning film *Dead Man Walking* has shed some light on this area. The question is no longer whether women can practice the "cure of souls," but to what point they already do. John Paul II gave a priestly example when he paid an amicable visit in prison to Mehmet Ali Agca, the man who wounded and tried to kill him. His faith told him that in so doing he was visiting Jesus. In the United States alone, there are already more than a hundred and thirty nuns and many other Catholic women serving as pastoral caregivers to convicted prisoners.

These women have proved themselves to be charismatically gifted reconcilers, healers, and preachers of the Good News. They perform their services with a specific mission from the Church. Meanwhile, it hasn't been quite three hundred years since the Roman Catholic Church finally made up its mind to allow consecrated virgins to teach various subjects, including religion, in school.

The development is truly breathtaking. Shortly after the end of the Council, I was invited to a general chapter of Dominican nuns. There I was asked by the superior general: "Where do you suppose we sisters will be in the foreseeable future?" My answer was: "In pastoral care for prisoners." In less than a decade, this superior was doing first social work and then pastoral care for prisoners. In addition, she is one of those prophetic women who has campaigned powerfully for a thorough reform of the penal system.

I would argue that the Church has already come a long way in the healthy process of reeducation. Now it will only take a relatively short step to the ordination of women priests who have already proved themselves as pastoral caregivers.

I cherish the bold hope that this unfortunate attempt at infallibilization, once the momentary astonishment it caused is over, can bring about two positive results: first, a more profound reflection on the doctrine of the infallibility of the pope and the Church as a whole; second, a more thorough explanation of the theological status of ordaining women. Beyond that, I suspect that throughout the Church more radical efforts will be made to avoid proclaiming important doctrines and decisions affecting the entire Church without paying due attention to women. There is still a great deal of catching up to do to compensate for the injustices, and to heal the wounds of the past.

The future of the transmission and deepening of faith largely depends upon the contribution of women. It also depends on the

6

118   MY HOPE FOR THE CHURCH

willingness of churchmen to ask for and gratefully accept this contribution. Feminist theology has a lot to say to us men as well. Our image of God should not be burdened with images of God stamped by the patriarchy. God is both fatherly grace and motherly tenderness. Inclusive language, important as it is, is not enough to express this.

The active presence of women in the Church and their thankful acceptance by everyone is part of healthy piety, of profound and unfalsified faith. We just have to let women tell us that after this setback suffered at the hands of the male magisterium. We have to inscribe it deeply into our own hearts. Future pastoral care should guarantee, above and beyond the domain of the family, that women caregivers can carry out their mission for the Church's understanding of the faith as fully as can men.

Naturally, it would be splendid if the pope were to realize and humbly acknowledge his error before he leaves us. I have spoken out on this several times: It would be a special sign of God's grace to ecumenism, if a pope, having made a glaring mistake, could just humbly acknowledge it. A friend once told me: "Only an incorrigible optimist like you would dare to hope for something like that." I ask the reader to pray with me for it.

The aura that still surrounds the pope, especially when he has his yeasayers all about him, makes it very difficult even for an otherwise holy individual sitting on the papal throne to confess his own errors and mistakes. It makes it difficult for him to go on learning and rethinking. A renewal of the understanding of the Petrine office must aim not only at ecumenical acceptability, but also at a holistic reshaping of the entire structure and atmosphere of the Church's leadership. That would make it relatively easier for a good pope to be ready to learn, to be able to rethink positions, and to admit his mistakes.

17

Celibacy and the Shortage of Priests

Existential Consternation

On this tricky question I know that I am not a neutral observer. I am doubly biased: I myself freely chose celibacy. I have lived a long lifetime as a celibate; and looking back I think that I have fared well with it.

The decision not to marry "for the sake of the kingdom of heaven" was by no means easy for me. It was clear to me that I was giving up something very beautiful and precious. It was likewise clear to me that I would have to reckon with the attractiveness of beautiful and noble women. Nevertheless, after careful reflection and prayer, I decided in favor of it. My main reason was the call that I felt to preach the glad tidings as a missionary. I found that reverence for women, for every woman, and vigilance over my motives were an effective aid against temptations. Giving myself credit for that would be foolish; and it would be twice as bad if, because of this experience, I were to look down on those who have had trouble with the law of celibacy.

This leads me to the second reason why I cannot consider myself a neutral observer: I have suffered enormously with others. I even think that this kind of suffering "got to me" much more than that which I went through with my own severe illnesses.

Let me cite just a few characteristic experiences: In Rome for many years, I helped and comforted a former monsignor. He suffered terribly from being excommunicated and from the impossibility of having a valid Catholic marriage with the mother of his nine children. For years, I regularly paid his medical and pharmaceutical bills. I was deeply moved when he told me once: "Perhaps this humiliation saved me. I was a proud prelate."

Quite a number of married—though not "validly" married—priests tried to follow along the path that in preconciliar days was the indispensable condition for being "laicized." They had to spend a year in total abstinence. Every single couple but one failed to make it. There were "backslidings" and tears (which I shared). I had stressed to the one successful couple that they had to be very tender with each other, and that advice helped.

A Carmelite nun once wrote me a letter, imploring me to talk her brother, a much loved and charismatic priest, out of asking for a dispensation to get married. She was convinced that he would listen to me. I met him, heard his story, and wept with him. They wanted to make him a bishop, but he saw no way out except marriage.

I spoke with Pope Paul VI about the whole issue in the first year of his pontificate. He was full of consternation and asked me to draw up a detailed memorandum. I argued that the response to all these cases had to be compassionate. In a great many of them, it is the unconditional duty of justice to offer speedy dispensations to priests who are obviously incapable of living a meaningful celibate life. They must be allowed to marry without any aftertaste of being "defrocked."

Nevertheless, at that time, I wasn't bold enough to say that such men, if otherwise they had all the qualities needed to do beneficial work, might be allowed to continue to function as priests. I did denounce the agreement between the Vatican and the government of Italy, whereby former priests could not be hired by the state.

For Pope Paul VI, the issue of laicization was a deeply felt concern. He was well aware that on his deathbed Pope John XXIII had voiced sadness over not having solved this thorny problem. At that point, dispensations were being handed out quickly, and one of the first to receive one was the abovementioned former monsignor with his nine children.

Whose heart wouldn't bleed to think that a Church law so contrary to the Gospel would help to cause so much pain? In the background stood a legalistic morality and an all-too-frequent recourse to punitive sanctions. In the twelfth century, when the popes set to work imposing universal celibacy, they didn't shy away from ordering recalcitrant wives of priests to be sold into slavery (to intimidate the others, of course). Weren't these churchmen themselves in a "Babylonian captivity" of legalistic thinking? Charism hardly blossoms in the shadow of a barbed-wire fence.

The Tragedy of the Pontificate of John Paul II

Here is a characteristic tragedy of the genially gifted and supremely zealous John Paul II. Shortly after his inauguration, he blocked all dispensations from priestly celibacy. Evidently, he was hoping that such legal rigor would bar the door to temptations against the law of celibacy. On the one hand the fact cannot be overlooked that the number of priests getting dispensations from celibacy (provided they gave up their priestly functions) was frighteningly high. On the other hand, I recall that many of my friends were quite shocked by the new pope's action. Sadly they voiced their fear that this would prove an omen for his entire pontificate. I tried to dissipate such fears, hoping that the pope would be willing to creatively rethink his decision. I had, after all, enthusiastically greeted the election of the "Polish pope." I had even predicted it to a Polish fellow Redemptorist.

After the inauguration of John Paul II, I met an old friend, Peter Hebblethwaite, on St. Peter's Square. A former Jesuit and a highly respected journalist, he asked me anxiously: "Aren't you worried that this very talented pope will turn out to be an authoritarian?" I answered: "I'm confident that his talent itself will protect him from that." For me it seemed obvious that the values of the Gospel can't be demanded or guarded by authoritarian means. The pope was calculating that harsh measures would stem the tide of flight from the celibate priesthood. I suspect that this made sense, more or less, for Poland. Excommunication still carried some social weight there. But infinitely more was at stake: the shining forth of a freely chosen and magnanimously lived charism throughout the world.

In this situation, the superiors of religious orders were soon in a panic. What were they supposed to do with their members who evidently weren't living, or had stopped living, the charism of celibacy for the kingdom of heaven? The Union of Superiors General in Rome sent a commission of three generals of religious orders to the pope to tell him plainly that their heart bled when their priests, after mature reflection, asked for a dispensation and then they didn't get one. Once married, they would automatically be excommunicated.

One of these three men told me a dramatic story. When they explained why they had come, the pope shot back: "You can go. I have formed my own conviction." What could they do except leave in disappointment?

After a few months, as the requests for dispensations kept piling up, the same three men were once again sent to the pope. This time they were told not to leave without at least presenting their concern in the name of the Union. Only when the pressure from many sides got still stronger could the pope be brought to change the order. For the most tragic cases at least the door was to be left slightly ajar, but I have been repeatedly told by those involved and by church superiors that the process of getting a dispensation, now as before, is extremely humiliating.

Still, Karol Wojtyla's calculation didn't work out at all. The number of requests for dispensations is just as high as it ever was. An unknown percentage of men don't bother with the procedure and remain technically in the "state of celibacy." But meanwhile they have given up any attempt to live the charism. Others wed outside the church in the more or less firm confidence that their marriage, despite laws to the contrary, counts as one in the eyes of God. I once heard a priest say: "God has blessed our marriage anyhow." One abyss calls to another.

I ask any priests and bishops who may read the following question: "What do you say to a pastor known as a beloved and zealous man, who confidentially reveals to you that he is living in what is for all practical purposes a marriage with a close woman friend? This man knows how to hide his tracks; and his conscience is convinced that in face of the Church's harsh rules it is better to "marry than to burn.""

Getting at the Root of the Problem

By now the number of requests for dispensations has, it is true, gone down somewhat. Many priests, of course, leave without asking for a dispensation, because they either can't cope with the procedure or simply reject it as unjust. But still more important is the fact that a great many suitable young men can't decide to ask for ordination. This is because of the harsh requirement of abstinence when priests attempt to get a dispensation. If it should prove impossible to live as celibates, they fear the sword of an unforgiving law.

Church authorities, too, have to study the issue of celibacy more thoroughly. Recently, an American publishing house asked me to review a book by A.W. Richard Sipe, *Celibacy: A Way of Loving, Living, and Serving* (Liguori/Triumph: Liguori, Mo., 1996). The author is a happily married man and father, a layman, a respected psychotherapist and theologian.

Layer by layer, he exposes the complex phenomenon of celibacy. Above all, he shows from his rich therapeutic experience that there are accessible paths to maturity in celibacy. Reading Sipe, one senses to what extent his love for truth and his love for human beings go hand in hand. His crucial point is: celibacy for the kingdom of heaven is a noble goal, and at the same time a process, a value that must always be realized more fully. It is a road, not a label or a static condition that one just adopts and that may later prove to be an inescapable trap. The author is a healer and religious caregiver through and through. He also knows how to encourage people to take the path of celibacy if they feel called to it. For me this book opens up a wholly different world and perspective from the one we see in the attempts to secure celibacy as a charism by laying on a thicker tangle of barbed wire.

Before moving on to further considerations, however, I would like to secure myself and the reader against the hopeless misunderstanding connected with the slogan "abolish celibacy." No person and no culture can abolish celibacy. There are and always will be men and women who for very different reasons freely renounce marriage or are forced to live as celibates against their will. One thinks of the many widows and widowers, the divorced people who can't find a partner or summon the courage to tie themselves down again. One thinks, too, of handicapped persons whom we could be helping better to cope with celibacy. In almost all cultures, celibacy is a many-sided phenomenon.

In the following reflections, I am primarily concerned with the relationship between charism, grace, and law in the lives of so-called "secular priests." They aim to live their priestly profession and their calling to holiness in the midst of the world. The basic question here is whether the "Latin" Church, the largest part of the Catholic Church, should continue to link admission to the priesthood with the obligation to celibacy.

Attempts at a Solution

One attempt—in many ways an obvious one—to answer this question points toward adopting, even if only with modifications, the traditional rule of the Orthodox and Uniate Eastern Churches: ordaining married men to the priesthood, while choosing bishops from the religious orders, where we find great respect for celibacy as freely lived in community.

Many years ago I knew a Hungarian bishop who belonged to the Uniates and who, while spending a long time under arrest under the Communists, had translated my *Law of Christ* into Hungarian. I asked him how things were going in his (Uniate) diocese with priestly vocations. He told me he had so many applicants but that he could admit at most a third of them. When I asked him about his criteria for selection, he promptly replied: I especially check whether the candidate has a good wife, someone who stands by him in human and pastoral affairs.

As a rule, the men ordained as priests in the Orthodox and Uniate Catholic Churches have already been married for some time. This avoids the understandable worry that priests might find themselves, so to speak, on the marriage market.

When the wife of an Orthodox priest dies or leaves him, the man knows that by choosing the priesthood he has obliged himself to live a life of celibacy for the sake of the kingdom of heaven.

At the same time in so doing he should and will serve to encourage the many persons who are compelled to live unmarried.

Nevertheless, I believe that in Orthodox Churches there has been careful consideration of whether this demand should always be imposed. One thinks, for example, of a priest whose wife dies when he is relatively young, leaving him with a lot of small children. It is true, the Orthodox Churches give their believers authoritative advice to accept celibacy in the case of the death of a first spouse or, particularly, of abandonment by a spouse. But this is always seen against the background of *oikonomia*, the virtue of the father of the house, who carefully determines what is the best for each individual case.

Thinking That Does Justice to History

Celibacy as a whole and especially the regulations for celibacy have a complex history. One thinks of the practice in Buddhism, where monks who have lived long years in contemplative retirement are expected later to bring these experiences into a full married life.

The imposition of celibacy on deacons and priests in the Latin Church was by no means a simple, linear development. The first attempts at legally requiring it go back to the fourth century. But it didn't generally prevail until the late Middle Ages. The social conditions and unfavorable evaluation of sexuality, even in marriage, made the imposition of celibacy easier.

At this time, the population of almost all the Western countries had reached a kind of limit. The number of independent peasants and artisans could scarcely be raised to any significant extent. Each family would have eight to ten births. Only one son and one daughter could hope to raise a family. Two to three children died in infancy. The rest might reside in the eldest brother's house or choose priestly or religious life, which gave them an automatic boost in social prestige. In a deeply religious environment, this form of celibacy was much more attractive than the celibacy of unmarried brothers and sisters who were mere family hangers-on.

One can say in general that until very recent times religious celibacy had a high degree of cultural acceptance. This was partly due to the fact that, despite the developing doctrine of the sacramentality of marriage, sex was viewed with many reservations. According to Augustine, marital intercourse was degrading in itself, redeemed only by the direct intention to procreate. Granted, this view was never the only one; but it was widely shared, especially by the clergy.

At the present time, the cultural situation is a far cry from medieval days. Among Christians, an explicitly positive appreciation of sexuality in marriage has prevailed, while at the same time the number of children born to married couples has plummeted. Economic conditions in postmodern society have gone through extraordinary changes from those of an agrarian social order. Consequently there is no available "surplus" of young people ready and suitable for celibacy. The time is gone forever when many young people could choose only between celibacy and life as an appendage to some relative's family. The Church must realize that the traditional reservoir for celibate priests has dried up.

Under these circumstances, the free choice of celibacy for the kingdom of heaven can become more explicit. But often we are talking about only a relatively small number of vocations.

I can illustrate this by my own experience: of my parents' twelve children, all of them very much wanted, two died in early childhood. The eldest fell as a soldier in World War I. The second eldest was released from a prisoner of war camp in poor health. One brother and one sister married. Six of us chose the profession of priest or religious life. None of the families of my great-nephews has more than three children.

One of the fundamental conclusions from these experiences and reflections is that doing "the same thing" under totally different circumstances changes the nature of "the same thing." Stubborn, literal clinging to the law of celibacy has long been a deliberate anachronism.

Everywhere people ask: how are things to continue? Our Church has already suffered enormously from being out of touch with its own time. The longer this goes on, the more overwhelming the consequences will be. Still, I take my stand with those who are deeply convinced that the pressure of historical conditions, with the help of public opinion, will bring change in the foreseeable future.

Indispensable Steps

A meaningful, enthusiastic solution of this and similar clusters of problems will likely never come until the necessary power is restored to the conferences of bishops and their regional assemblies. This restoration must be in keeping with the old Catholic principle of subsidiarity.

My own expectations look roughly like this: there are regions, though their number is decreasing, where priestly celibacy had and still has a high degree of acceptance. And in such places, thanks to a favorable environment, there are also enough suitable celibate vocations. But one can't overlook the fact that there are also regions where celibate vocations are lacking or priestly celibacy as a strictly controlled law is not producing good results. The welfare of the Church and the basic right of all Catholic communities to regular eucharistic celebrations and a consecrated pastoral caregiver are vital needs in this case. They unconditionally demand that God's mandate and Jesus' testament should never be sacrificed to a purely human law, however venerable.

One first step will likely be the *consecration of tested men* (*viri probati*), that is, men who have already proved themselves in the Church's service and either have the necessary theological and pastoral education, or who are ready and willing to acquire it. The ordination of women will probably not be possible for some time yet. But all steps that are already conceivable should be taken to get capable women—and there are such women everywhere— to participate in pastoral care. Many positions, such as parish advisers, have already worked out well. Women active in the "cure of souls" must be allowed to introduce their charisms into the totality of the Church's pastoral care.

In my opinion, there are no serious theological obstacles to entrusting suitable women ministers right now with the task of administering baptism or celebrating the sacraments of reconciliation and the anointing of the sick. Any theological reservations on this account, as far as the Church worldwide is concerned, should be swept away.

Next we come to the question of how to help priests who can no longer live a meaningful, productive celibate life without simply renouncing their priestly service. I like to imagine that bishops and their advisers could first of all clarify the issue of whether individual priests, apart from their problems with celibacy, have what it takes to render useful priestly service. In all likelihood a sabbatical year to think things over would not only be accepted, but welcomed, by many priests.

A most important first step will be the ordination of tested parish leaders. In Africa, these are often called simply "catechists," although they bear almost all the responsibility for whole parishes. These men, who are distinguished by rich pastoral experience and often by great skill, have long been regularly celebrating the solemn liturgy of the word and afterward a moving communion service. Once a month they generally take a long bicycle trip to pick up preconsecrated hosts from a priest. One needn't be a prophet to foresee that this will change as soon as centralism gives way to a church constitution based on subsidiarity.

One has all the more reason to hope that this will happen soon once all responsible church leaders have realized one thing: it is a serious case of *heteropraxis* (an act of ingrained heresy) when, for the sake of the historically conditioned law of celibacy, the fundamental legacy and right of the Christian community to regular celebration of the Eucharist is violated. All the clergy share in the responsibility that this basic law not be institutionally violated, with a "good conscience," as it were.

Another significant step would be if all of us who have bound ourselves voluntarily to celibacy for the kingdom of heaven were to live our charism gratefully and joyfully, with a readiness to make sacrifices. Then this vocation would strike others as really attractive.

Reintegrating Men Who Have Left the Priesthood

Once the steps mentioned above have been taken, the Church in the various parts of the world can speedily turn to the long-standing problems of reintegrating priests who have come to grief because of celibacy or of the ways the law of celibacy has been implemented. Many of those who have freely renounced, or were forced to abandon, their priestly service due to celibacy had and have priestly qualities in a high degree—perhaps in an even higher degree than others with prestigious places in the hierarchy.

The reader will presumably be familiar, as I am, with several married priests who have left only on account of the law of celibacy, but who otherwise have all the necessary virtues. Many have gone back to continue, one way or another, in Church service, for example as religion teachers. They are allowed to do everything that women can do; and they are forbidden only what women in Church service are normally forbidden. On the other hand, many others are completely active in serving the Church, although they fail to meet some crucial conditions.

How are things with their celibacy? Here is a drastic example: One day I saw a fancy Cadillac parked in the inner court of the Accademia Alfonsiana. When I asked a highly esteemed colleague to whom it belonged, he answered ironically: "Don't you know? That belongs to the bride of a powerful monsignor." Haven't some well set-up priests chained themselves to this sort of "concubinage" out of the posturings of power, ambition, or greed, to name only a few motivation?

Once celibacy has ceased to be the main criterion for admission to and membership in the priesthood, our demands will, on the whole, turn out to be much higher and more consistent. There are priests who after leaving the service of the Church have remained loyal, despite the unfair treatment they have received. Some of these have even made a mark for themselves through their active participation in the life of the Church. Obviously, such persons are on the whole suitable for full priestly service. When the problem of ordaining "tested men" has been solved, it shouldn't be too hard to reintegrate many of the priests who left simply because of celibacy, especially if they are living in good marriages.

All that can proceed organically, if the "barbed wire" of legalism has disappeared from all our heads, and we have once again gotten an unimpeded view both of the calling of priests and of the charism of celibacy. One can see in the face and the whole bearing of some ex-priests that they are still priestly persons. Many could return to work as priests, enriched now by experience, and even more spiritually mature.

18

Changes in the Pastoral Care of the Divorced

This burning issue has already been dealt with in the first part of this book. Here the emphasis lies on the dynamism of change that is, on the whole, a powerful presence already. The fronts that have hardened at the moment should not discourage us. A painful threshold seems to have been crossed now, and in such a way that we can see the turnaround taking place more clearly here than in any other problem area.

The basic attitude toward issues of pastoral care for the divorced is a kind of shibboleth. It allows us to draw revealing conclusions about people's underlying image of God, their understanding of humanity, their interpretation of the Gospel, and, not least of all, the way they look at the relationship between grace (the Gospel) and law. It is not surprising that, on these matters also, opinions differ in terms of ecumenical perspective.

Seldom in the history of vital issues in the Church has the virtue of *epieikeia* (interpreting a law by its spirit rather than the letter) been so inconspicuous as in the position taken by Pope John Paul II. He seems not even to acknowledge it as a virtue, simply to fear it as an excuse.

Just as in the Orthodox Churches of the East, Western Christianity applied *epieikeia* to the pastoral care of the divorced up until the twelfth century. This development was in large part due to the influence of the Irish and Scottish Church.

Only with Pope Alexander III (1159–1181) did a harder line in treating divorced and remarried persons emerge. As a practical matter, this meant that divorced people who remarried while their first wife or husband was still alive were banned from receiving the sacraments until they did harsh penance.

Two points should be considered here. First, in the age of the patriarchal extended family, divorced persons were not, as they are today, scattered like sand, left hopelessly alone. As a matter of course, they were integrated back into the family of their origins. Second, in the total cultural picture at that point in time perseverance in marriage was basically an achievement of a given social milieu. The irrevocable breakup of a marriage meant a personal failure on the part of those concerned.

Today the situation is all but reversed. Success in marriage makes high personal demands on couples. The overall structure of society "explains" marital collapse. In the old days, the average duration of a marriage was around twenty years, today it is approaching fifty years. That, too, explains the heightened demands on people's capacity to persevere.

In the modern urbanized world, divorced people are cast about and exposed to many dangers. In addition, they are by no means a marginal problem anymore. In most countries around a third of marriages go hopelessly under. The lonely divorced person is very often exposed to heavy mental and moral burdens. An old insight is especially relevant here: to urge the same standard under radically changed living conditions turns out to mean something very different from what it used to.

The altered social and cultural situation, the great progress made in biblical studies, better knowledge of the history and variety of cultures, the ecumenical coming together of Churches—all this has led to a significant transformation in Catholic theology and pastoral practice. Everywhere we find at least tentative moves toward a more discriminating kind of thinking and action to match it.

This could be seen at the Bishops Synod in 1980 regarding questions of the family. Two important petitions came to a vote and received almost unanimous approval. The first proposal stressed the strict duty to think and act more sensitively in the pastoral care of the divorced. The second urgently requested the pope to see to it that our Church show more willingness to learn in the face of the long tradition of the Orthodox Church, especially its spirituality and practice of *oikonomia*.

In Western tradition, the virtue of *epieikeia* roughly corresponds to the Orthodox *oikonomia*, although the latter has a wider and deeper range. The synodal fathers who voted for the two proposals were quite obviously, if not uniquely, concerned about having a more diversified standard for admitting people to the Eucharist.

In his concluding address, the pope surprised the synod's participants with a strange across-the-board requirement:

> If both partners for serious reasons…cannot comply with the obligation to separate, they take on themselves the duty to live in complete continence, that is, to refrain from all acts proper to married couples.
>
> (*Familiaris Consortio*, Nov. 1981, n. 84).

Over the whole course of the synod not a word had been spoken about such a demand. It earned the pope some vehement criticism. Nevertheless, in the years that followed, its harsh terms were repeated again and again: total abstinence as a precondition for the receiving of communion by all divorced and remarried persons. Not only those immediately involved, but psychotherapists and many spiritual advisers warned that this would condemn second marriages to failure as well.

Understandably, developments in pastoral care led to various approaches and attempts to deal with the issue of divorced Catholics. That is how we must view the venture by the three bishops from the Upper Rhine (Saier, Lehmann, and Kasper): a careful set of instructions for discriminating reflection and action on this thorny issue.

The three bishops had almost all the theologians, not least of all the pastoral theologians, on their side, although naturally not everyone had the nerve to speak out. On the other hand, quite a few voices were raised chiding the three bishops for being too hesitant. Some said that in their praiseworthy efforts to offer a discriminating standard the bishops had drawn the limits of *epieikeia* much too narrowly.

The Vatican took an altogether different view. On three occasions the bishops had to journey to Rome for questioning. Finally the pope's answer arrived. It essentially said: "No exceptions." There could be no *epieikeia* or any application of *oikonomia*. Even if the couples and their spiritual advisers were convinced that the failed marriage lacked "validity," the individuals were absolutely excluded from the sacraments unless they renounced all conjugal acts. In all cases, the decision of the marriage tribunal (*rota*) was definitive. Thus did the practice and virtue of *epieikeia* fell completely by the wayside.

At this point, readers may perhaps ask me how, despite everything, I still maintain that a turnaround for the better is in the offing. I have many reasons for my prognosis. Above all, I would mention the dignified, upright, and absolutely nonviolent attitude of the three German bishops and the encouraging echoes of their action: there was an international wave of sympathy in response to it. And so the difficult question of pastoral care for the divorced has reached a wholly new degree of attention.

I admire the courage, but not the wisdom, of the pope in his unlimited zeal for the controlled and controlling application of his doctrines and decisions. No doubt he is following his conscience. Of course, that conscience is shaped by a specific tradition and mode of thinking. More and more one hears the question as to whether or not popes have a harder time than ordinary mortals when it comes to changing their mind. The current papal practice in doctrine and discipline is painting itself into a corner. But the urgent signs of the times admonish us to greater openness in thinking and dialogue. They bid us to engage in emphatically ecumenical thinking, in collective fidelity to the compassionate practice and teaching of Christ. We all still have a lot to learn.

The pope feels unconditionally obliged to defend the holiness of the sacrament of marriage. The tragic part is that he is taking as his point of departure a preconciliar understanding of the sacramentality of marriage. That view treated the *marriage contract*, in which both spouses confer on each other the "exclusive right to acts that are by nature oriented to procreation" as the *sacrament of marriage*. That way the sacrament becomes a sword of Damocles hanging over the heads of the divorced.

There can be no doubt that the Second Vatican Council abandoned this notion once and for all. The Council says: "The intimate community of life and love, founded by the Creator and safeguarded by its own laws, is…established…by the bond of marriage. This intimate union, as a mutual donation of persons, along with the welfare of the children, calls for the unconditional fidelity of the spouses and demands indissoluble unity" (*GS* n. 49).

In this same perspective, the Orthodox and Reformed Churches likewise unanimously emphasize that the spouses have to do everything possible to safeguard the bond of love and life. For its part, the Church must also do everything to prevent a breakdown of the marriage. But if the formal legal contract as such were the sacrament, then every marriage, as a sacrament, even after it had permanently collapsed, would mean an inexorable ban on entering any new marriage.

In contrast, what if sacramentality, following the viewpoint of the Council and the parts of Christendom separated from Rome, were to be seen from the standpoint of the bond of life and love? In that case, once there has been an absolutely hopeless breakdown in the marriage, it no longer makes sense to speak of a marriage. To be sure, a whole series of duties persist. One can't simply erase the tragic past. But as a "sacrament," the "dead" marriage no longer unconditionally stands in the way of a new marriage, because the core of sacramentality is seen in the "bond of life and love."

In this debate also, as on the question of ordaining women and the supposedly intrinsic evil of contraception, we see looming once again the double problem of reception or nonreception. On all these issues, which he has treated with such urgency, Pope John Paul II never "received" the statements of the Council, the findings of current theological research, or the clear indications from the people of God about their sense of the faith. The unavoidable reverse side of this is the nonreception by the people of God of firm papal teachings. Obsolescent models of thought cannot prevail against new findings and viewpoints. "The future has already begun."

This experience finds a voice, for example, in the wishes of the laity in many countries. One welcomes the frankness and nonviolence which are features of this process of replacing old thought models with emerging new viewpoints. A common learning experience has been set in motion that forms the basis for our hope that in the future the Church will be better prepared to face controversial issues and to more readily interpret the signs of the times.

I share the hopes of many others that the Roman Catholic Church, including the pope, will summon the courage and humility to learn from the long-tried and tested practice of the Orthodox Churches on the question of *oikonomia* and in many other matters. Then the service of Saint Peter within the Catholic Church and the whole ecumene will also be a true service of the *servus servorum Christi*.

Notes

1. *Es geht auch anders, Plädoyer für eine neue Umgangsform in der Kirche* (Freiburg, 1994).
2. Düsseldorf, 1934ff.
3. In all this, I am not the only moral theologian who after the experience of the Council, and very consciously in keeping with its directives, strove to let myself be led above all by the Spirit and the statements of holy Scripture. Cf. on this point the essay of an exegete, Michael Clark, "The Major Scriptural Themes in the Moral Theology of Father Bernard Häring," *Studia Moralia* 30 (1992), 3–16; 277–87.
4. Even in the Church this liberation, in all its breadth and depth, depends upon whether we can radically free ourselves from the consequences of patriarchalism. There is much that might be said about this. I refer to G. Baudler's *Gott und Frau. Die Geschichte der Gewalt, Sexualität und Religion* [*God and Woman: The History of Violence, Sexuality, and Religion*] (Munich, 1991).
5. Cf. the excellent book by E. A. Stadter, *Wenn du wüßtest, was ich fühle. Einführung in die Beziehungstherapie* [*If You Knew What I Feel: Introduction to Relationship Therapy*] (Freiburg, 1992).
6. *Lexikon für Theologie und Kirche*, 2nd ed., Vol. 12: *Das Zweite Vatikanische Konzil. Dokumente und Kommentare*, Part I, 227.
7. Munich, 1967/72,
8. Göttingen, 1987.
9. London, 1987.
10. Paderborn, 1991.
11. Published in *Moral Theology: Challenge for the Future, Festschrift for Richard A. McCormick* (New York, 1990), pp. 213–214.
12. On this whole complex, see my article, *"Christliche Ethik im ökumenischen Dialog"* ["Christian Ethics in Ecumenical Dialogue"] in KNA, ÖKUMENISCHE INFORMATION, N. 18, April 29, 1992, 5–10; and n. 19, May 6, 1992, 5–15.

Index

1912–1998